MW01268512

A Daughter's Hero

**Vietnam
1968-1970**

A Tribute to a Veteran of Vietnam

Julius "Jerry" Duane Weber

A Daughter's Hero

by

Julie K. Weber-Torres

To Billy & Carol
God bless you!
Love!
Julie K Weber Torres
11-4-14

Introduction

I feel compelled to share the life of my dad, Julius "Jerry" Duane Weber, a Vietnam War Veteran. My dad is truly my hero. He certainly lived an eventful life during his fifty-five years. He was a selfless person who always helped others in need even if he went without. My uncle always said when my dad had a dollar, you had fifty cents. From my dad, I learned that we should cherish our journey through this life. I believe that we should not take our days on earth for granted and we need to continuously seek out happiness every day. Life is truly a gift! I decided to share his life with others for several reasons, but most importantly to help others. I've never written a book in my life; so I did have to collaborate with another writer to assist me with the first draft to structure the book effectively. I must point out that this book was not written to humiliate or cause any embarrassment to anyone, especially my dad. This is my personal interpretation of events that includes my own feelings, memories, conclusions and opinions based on what I have discovered, learned or experienced throughout the years. I've been asked from others how long this book took to me write. Well, I guess I can say that I've been writing it all of my life.

Dad and I did not talk about his time in Vietnam extensively. In fact, dad never opened up completely with anyone about his war experience. He buried the memories deep inside. When he said anything it was brief.

Throughout the book, I will share a vivid collection of his mini conversations that he had with others over the years. One of my brothers thought that dad kept Vietnam a secret. A wife of a Vietnam Veteran told me that she didn't think any of the Veterans spoke about it much. Since my dad didn't, I was never completely aware of the impact of him being in a war and what it could have on a person, but now I can only look back, research and speculate on what experiences he went through in Vietnam and how it shaped his life with us, the family he formed after returning from the war. I see many connections I did not make over the years, connections that make his later life more understandable to those of us who knew and loved him and suffered watching his demise.

Something else that struck me as I conducted research on the Vietnam War and the men and women who served there: how much of a debt we owe them. How they put their lives on the line and suffered unspeakable horrors for the sake of other people's freedom, to fight a "proxy" war in the worldwide struggle between democracy and communism. When I read about the war protestors here in America and the men and women over in Nam, I could not help but feel the incredible heroism of those who went over there to a small, incomprehensible country from a large and largely unsupportive country, when it was not "cool" to go and be a soldier in that particular war. When I read their stories of humor, valor, suffering, death and fear, I know who the cool ones really were—the men and women who went to Vietnam. They've never been honored enough for the down to earth bravery they showed in facing death every day, far-far from home. One Veteran who served with my dad tells me they took mortar fire every single night. That was his life for two long years. He paid a great psychological price for it—some of the uncounted costs of war. One day my dad was at my house visiting and I shared a photograph of a young Vietnamese girl with him and he looked at me through an empty stare asking me where I got it from. I said that I didn't know but, I had it for several years. Nothing else was said and I put the picture away. That was one of the few brief conversations related to Vietnam that we spoke of together. I guess I was uncomfortable with trying to discuss his experience or afraid to upset him.

Thankfully, my grandma and aunt saved several of dads Vietnam photographs that he mailed home while serving in Vietnam. This made research a bit easier since, he wrote details on the back and front of some of the photos. I don't know if dad knew that they kept his photographs over the years or not. I recently discovered that his brother kept several of dad's photo slides from Vietnam. He had several slides displaying the horror and death experienced in the war. He said that dad took and destroyed the gory slides without him knowing. He believes dad was trying to abolish the gruesome memories of Vietnam?

My dad served in the United States Army from March 8, 1968 to October 11, 1970. He was sent to Vietnam as a Light Equipment Engineer assigned to the 557th Engineer Company in August 1968. The unit was so small that it was often attached to other units to provide direct support. I'm told that attaching to other units caused them to not get credit or appropriate recognition. At times the guys were put on the front lines to help provide combat support and engaged in firefights. It also happened while standing guard at the base camps.

I read that the mission of the engineers in Vietnam changed in the year 1969. Instead of providing only military support, the engineers were to build highways, schools and various infrastructures as a way of nation building so that the Vietnamese could stand on their own. These efforts of the engineers left the country of Vietnam with a road system that benefited them economically and with many structures that they could not have achieved on their own. In addition to our efforts to prevent a communist takeover, the United States left a legacy of benevolent works in the nation of Vietnam.

Another 557ᵗʰ Engineer told me that they named their equipment "Dust Eaters" originally. They later named the equipment "Earth Eaters". The name was given due to the fact that the dirt would blow upward causing the equipment operator to consume a lot of the dirt as they worked

In early 1968, my dad decided to go and visit an Army Recruiting Station located in Rhinelander, Wisconsin to join the Army. He was only seventeen years old. He volunteered to join the Army and go to

Vietnam to serve our country. Joining the service during wartime was a common family tradition. I guess he thought it was his turn to go? My grandparents were required to sign a consent form to authorize him to join the service since he was underage. My dad was quickly ordered to Vietnam after he completed his specialized training. My grandmother then regretted signing the consent form, fearing he wouldn't make it back home alive. I hear his grandparents feared losing him every day he was gone. He was certainly their pride and joy.

Dad was a courageous person and a risk taker as I knew him later in life. He always stood up for whatever he believed in. Enlisting in the service during war time certainly was an act of true patriotism for any age, especially a seventeen year old. He was awarded several medals for serving in the Army during the Vietnam War. I never saw any of his original medals- only a dog tag, so I requested and received replacement medals by contacting the National Personnel Records Center. The Army Commendation Medal was presented to my dad who distinguished himself by exceptionally meritorious service in support of military operations against communist aggression in the Republic of Vietnam during September 1968 - October 1970. He astutely surmounted extremely adverse conditions to obtain consistently superior results. Through diligence and determination he invariably accomplished every task with dispatch and efficiency. His unrelenting loyalty, initiative and perseverance brought him

wide acclaim and inspired others to strive
for maximum achievement. Selflessly working
long and arduous hours, he has contributed
significantly to the success of the allied
effort. His commendable performance was in
keeping with the finest traditions of the
military service and reflects distinct
credit upon himself and the United States
Army. The National Defense Service Medal
was awarded to all active duty in the
United States military during specific
dates of service. My dad also received a
Vietnam Service Medal with 2 bronze stars &
one Silver Star attachment. The stars were
authorized to military personnel for each
qualifying campaign. Dad participated in
seven different campaigns during his time
in Vietnam. Another award was the Republic
of Vietnam Campaign Ribbon w/device known

as the "1960 Bar". The bar displays the
date 1960 followed by a dash and a blank
space. This was caused by the government of
the Republic of Vietnam stating the 1960
bar would show the dates of the Vietnam War
from start to finish, with the ending date
placed on the bar after the South
Vietnamese had triumphed over North
Vietnamese. Since the South fell in April
1975, and the government ceased to exist,
an ending date for the 1960 bar was never
established. The American military departed
from Vietnam in March 1973 after the peace
settlement was signed earlier that year and
U.S. Congress stopped funding the war.

The United States of America was no
longer involved in the war after 1973.

In March 1968 dad's journey began as he
arrived at Fort Campbell, Kentucky for his

(BCT) Basic Combat Training and then in May 1968 he was transferred to Fort Dix, New Jersey to (AIT) Advanced Individual Training to learn the skills needed to perform his job. The initial course of study was a Wheel Vehicle Mechanic. This was to handle the maintenance and repair of light and heavy tactical vehicles and selected armored vehicles. He received additional training as a General Vehicle Repairman in July 1968. In January 1969 he was listed as an Engineer Equipment Mechanic and lastly an Engineer Equipment Repairman by July 1969. His starting rank was a Private E-1 which was a very low rank in the military and his highest rank attained was a Specialist 5, which was an E-5.

Aerial view of Vietnam

Throughout my research I discovered that
dads unit the 557th LE Engineering Company
was one of many units exposed to Agent
Orange, a toxic blend of herbicides. The
U.S. military sprayed millions of gallons
on the trees and vegetation that provided
cover for enemy forces. Later we found that
the chemicals sprayed caused many Vietnam
Veterans and their families, as well as the
Vietnamese population serious health
issues. I know my dad developed several

health conditions following his service but, issues related to Agent Orange are not proven to be service connected at this time. I do know he was certainly exposed to the traumatic stress that would mark his life ever afterward and cause him to embark on a life of alcoholism. I genuinely associate dad's continuous struggles with alcohol due to his time served in the Vietnam War.

I've been told that dad returned home from Vietnam not only a man, but a changed man. Relatives say that he seemed to be always on guard and angry as hell at times. He would often awaken from sleep ready to fight, was he sleeping on a hair-trigger, transported back into a combat zone in Vietnam?

Many came back changed, especially the
ones who worked in the midst of danger
zones. Most of them were young, early
twenties—and they faced existential
questions of life and death, courage and
cowardice, grief and loss, as well as
victory and exhilaration in the few years
of their service, more than most of us face
in a lifetime.

Arthur Varanelli, Vietnam Veteran:

"I took my Vietnam battlefield experiences
and put them in a box, so to speak, and
tied down the lid with locks and chains. I
did this in an attempt to forget the whole
thing and never have to deal with it again.
It did not work...These raw memories of my
experiences were corrosive and leaked out
of the box disconnectedly, resulting in
behaviors, feelings and experiences that

were inexplicable, not grounded in the
present reality of things, and very much
unlike my behaviors in my pre-Vietnam
life...

If people you trust tell you that you are
out of line, very different from what
people know of you before your combat
experience, please believe what these
people are telling you! Your behavior might
include becoming 'an angry person' for no
apparent reason; being intrigued with what
it is like to die or wanting to join fallen
friends; becoming aimless; using risk or
the power of authority to get that
adrenalin boost to counter depression;
literally flashing back in time and space
to where you see, feel and smell things
that are ordinary or extraordinary; and
other like things. If this is the case, and

people you trust are worried about you, head for the closest medical professional skilled in the diagnosis and management of PTSD (Post-Traumatic Stress Disorder) and get checked out."

http://www.pbs.org/pov/regardingwar/converstions/coming-home/post-traumatic-stress-disorder-ptsd-par, accessed December 11, 2010

The changed man who returned from Vietnam was the only one I knew—and in spite of his faults and flaws, I loved him deeply and always-always will. He was a good-natured person who would embrace others by positioning his arms around their neck and telling them how much he loved them anytime and anywhere. He enjoyed being surrounded by his family and friends. He had a wonderful sense of humor and could tell endless jokes and stories. Dad was a genuine guy who believed in people and would stand up for you. He wanted the best for others. He will always be my hero for fighting the good fight in Vietnam and battling the demons that assailed him after he came back. Unable to forget the horrid memories, he carried the war with him for 35 long years. It is to him and to all the Veterans who fought in that war including the families and friends who have suffered from the effects of any war, alcoholism or PTSD that I dedicate this book in hopes of creating some kind of understanding.

It is also a memorial to a great man—my hero—my dad.

Chapter One: The Early Years

My dad is having some fun in this photo taken in Vietnam, but the bottle was to become too much of a source of comfort in his life

Turning to alcohol to forget the fear, loss and pain they encountered in the war and at home was so common, that ads offered assistance to Vietnam Veterans for Post-Traumatic Stress Disorder asked the question "Are you drinking to try to forget?" In this picture, dad is goofing off in Vietnam, but this could have been a prophecy that the bottle would mean too much to him in his post-Vietnam years.

Interestingly I found, the soldiers were to some extent supplied with basic needs, except during incursions into Cambodia, which Veterans assured me they were poorly supplied with food. At times some veterans say they ate leftover World War II c-rations. I hear that during dry seasons the Engineers were unable to even take showers. They would go several weeks at a time, especially when they worked out in the field away from their base camp.

The men relied on the bonds of buddies as one of its greatest assets in the field. Out there, there was no one to rely on but the man next to you. I guess the beer sometimes made the friendships flow a little better and eased the tension of the constant danger. They also hugged each other at times, because they never knew if that person would be alive tomorrow or not.

It was like knowing you were going to die, but didn't know when.

After the war, some Vietnam Veterans went numb emotionally to stop feeling the pain; others turned to the bottle. They experienced the anguish of watching buddies die in pain, their bodies torn and decimated and the frustration of an enemy who never stood and fought but ambushed and harassed and bombed at night. "The night," a veteran assures me, "belonged to Charlie" (Charlie was the nickname American soldiers gave to the Vietcong). The enemy might be looking out at you from the eyes of a villager who just did your laundry for you but was really an informant for the Viet Cong. The soldiers said they could not even trust the children. Sometimes they carried explosives and they would set them off inside the American Army camps. Playing on the sympathy and affection the American soldiers had for children, sometimes they would enter camp, beg for candy, and then set off explosives or even steal from the soldiers. My brother recalls a story that dad told him about not being able to trust the children. One day dad was slowly driving down a road, likely to avoid exploding a mine and a kid appeared out of nowhere and jumped up to steal a carton of his cigarettes off of his dashboard. Dad reacted by shooting his gun to scare off the kid. He knew he wasn't an enemy, but only a crook. I hear dad felt sorry for the children in Vietnam and was bothered that they suffered so much during the war.

Not being able to fully trust the villagers, even the children, added to the stress of serving in Vietnam.

My dad was not a person who was capable of turning himself numb to overcome all of the stress. He loved people too much. He loved life too much. So he drank to medicate his pain and endless horrid memories.

My parents met each other only months after he came home from Vietnam. While dating their relationship was decent between them but, she noticed that he was a heavy drinker. She said he used to go out with his friends and family to the bars and get into some horrific fights. He would come home and tell her that he was afraid because he would beat people up so bad that he didn't know if they survived or not. His violent tendencies caused her to break up with him and move away out of state. Of course, he ran after her asking for her to move back, so she gave him another chance. Soon they got married. After they got married she says that's when all hell broke loose. They had four children together but, you can say they really had five children because my mother already had my oldest brother from a previous marriage. My parents' marriage ended within nine years due to his alcoholism, which led to frequent eruptions of verbal and physical abuse. She says their marriage wasn't a rosy one and it was a living nightmare at times. A lot of what happened she can't even remember because she thinks she had a mental breakdown at some point. Mom says their relationship was really bad and that she tried to suppress the memories. She does recall smoking about five packs of cigarettes a day due to the overwhelming stress. At times she feared for her own life and thought if they stayed together that one of them would have been killed.

One night she was beat up badly and afterward he brought her a 357 magnum and asked her to kill him. She said that she grabbed the gun and laid it on the counter and said," I'm not like you Jerry"! "I'm not the abusive one!" Did he do this because of the guilt and shame he was feeling for abusing her? Did he really want to die? Was this his way of saying that he was sorry? Was he just incapable of controlling his temper? Was this anger triggered by the horrible memories in Nam?

I know they tried several times to stay together, but things never changed. She would stay at times because she loved him and thought she could change him.

Obviously, she would not be able to do so. She went on to share another incident. She told me that while on vacation visiting family our dad came home from the bar quite intoxicated and started a fight with her in front of his family. My mom ended up grabbing a hammer and hit him on top of his head to get him off of her. This caused him to stumble around for bit confused or shocked but, her violent action ended the fight.

Another time, my older brothers and I woke to hearing mom crying and shouting so, we called the police for help. We certainly were afraid to be the one who called the police, but figured that dad wouldn't know who did it and besides that, the call needed to be made to end the violence and protect our mom from further abuse. I didn't know at the time why he got so enraged to do the things he did.

Recently, I asked mom if he shared any stories with her about his experience in Vietnam. She said he talked very little about his time there, but he had weak moments and would open up about it. She found a picture of a beautiful Vietnamese woman one day and asked about her. He told her that they dated each other in Nam and her name was pronounced "Tree" in English.

He met her during R&R (Rest & Relaxation) the time off earned while serving in Nam. He said that they spent time together but, often he was run off by the Vietnam Army. She doesn't remember any other details about their relationship.

He told her that he drove an earth scraper and the Vietnamese would run out in front of them to throw hand grenades while they worked and the Vietnamese would get themselves killed. She said that the guys over there feared for their lives all of the time. The men worked countless hours. Dad would talk in his sleep at night and would at times speak another language which, she says it sounded Vietnamese. My brother heard it before too. Mom recalled, dad telling her about a story about when he was leaving Nam to return back home. A bomb exploded when he and some other soldiers were waiting to fly out. He was sitting on his locker when the explosion hit. It caused some shrapnel to hit his stomach and left him with small scars. He says he was luckier than some of the others. I'm sure this traumatic incident caused thoughts of guilt for surviving when others so close to him did not? He said that Vietnam had a horrible stench in the air. He developed problems with his feet while being in Nam which he called "Jungle Rot". It is a foot fungus caused by prolonged exposure to damp, unsanitary conditions. Often our soldiers waded through water following monsoon periods. On October 6th, 1968 dad received medical care for nodular lesions on his feet. The pain was so severe that he was unable to sleep. Later in life, I remember taking him to the store to buy different products for his feet so; the foot fungus must have stayed with him.

As difficult as my parent's life was at times, my mom assures me that there were special moments spent together too and that he was good to her at times throughout their relationship. They went on vacations and had fun times together. He worked 3rd shift most of the time, so he would be home for dinners during the week and they'd relax and watch movies together. He worked on different projects around the house, especially with the cars or on his motorcycles. Most weekends were when he would take off to go drinking. Sometimes he would not return home until after the weekend was over. If he stayed home on the weekend things would often get out of control with partying. Throughout all the heartache she still loved him. My mom thinks that their marriage would have survived if only he could have stopped drinking. She asked him and even begged him to stop drinking several times but, he just drank more. Still today she says that she has never loved any man more than him. I can say that my mom is an amazingly strong woman with a forgiving heart but, ultimately she decided to end their relationship. She couldn't deal with the continuous problems anymore.

During their divorce, I remember my mom trying her best to stay involved with church. My mom even convinced dad to attend one time as a condition for her to move us back into his house. The agreement was not for them to reconcile, but only to have the family together. I remember sitting in church anticipating his arrival. I really wanted him to come because then we would get to live together again. In the middle of the service he walked in, wearing his blue jeans, winter coat jacket and cowboy boots. I remember that the preacher brought dad straight to the altar as he entered the room and prayed over him. The whole church was praying for him too at this time. It was a powerful moment and I was crying tears of joy, especially relieved that he even showed up. I was proud of him for coming to church to put together our family again. This was a big moment! That was the one and only time he ever attended church with us. According to his military records he was listed as a Lutheran. Also, I hear that his grandfather was also a devoted Lutheran and that there is a church pew dedicated in his memory still today.

Dad had a loving heart but, he lived on the edge too much. Here's one little example from long ago when I was a child. After leaving my uncle and aunt's house, my dad was driving and my younger brother was in the back yelling: "Drive fast! Drive faster!" Of course, he put the pedal to the metal and he was then pulled over by the police to get a speeding ticket. That was not the first, nor the last time he would be accosted by police for demonstrating his wild side.

I remember when I was about eight years old a little girl slapped me in the face as I walked home from school one day and I ran home crying. My dad was working on his car and he quickly ran towards me asking what was wrong. I told him that a girl slapped me and he went running down the street screaming at the girl for hitting me. He was protective over his family or friends.

Wild or not, at the same time, he was a generous, hard-working man. My great aunt told me that dad started working at a young age. She had watched my dad work outside during the cold winter months in Wisconsin, when the land was buried in snow. While dad was in the Army, she said he even helped support the family while he was away. I hear he was an avid reader as a youngster and would close down the libraries reading. I'm told he took after his grandma in that she would offer food to people in need and invite strangers over for supper. People remember my dad as being a lovable and caring person his whole life.

While dad was in Vietnam he mailed his aunt a greeting card following the birth of her first child, which she still has today. The card read "CONGRATULATIONS on your latest development!" He wrote, "Hope you and the baby are ok. I just got the letter today from Nora that you had your baby. Hope you'll name him after grandpa. Was sure glad to hear you had a boy. Signed.. Lots of Luck and Love -Jerry." He was always close with all of his family. I heard that his grandma and grandpa were worried sick waiting for him to return from Vietnam.

Some of my happiest early memories were when my dad's family would come over to visit, or when we went to their houses. As a child I had a great time playing with all my cousins while the adults hung out, playing country music like Waylon Jennings while some had beverages.

Later in life, I knew my dad as to some extent a workaholic, a proud union pipe fitter, an excellent welder, and one of the best at his job because he took such pride in doing it well. He enjoyed his work with the union and often encouraged other family and friends to join too.

He was very generous to those around him and helped out financially when he could. Material items didn't matter. His motto was "Never have more than you can carry." I'm sure he learned part of that motto being in Vietnam. What the soldiers could carry on them was very important to them. They had to be careful on how much they weighed because they moved around so much. They carried items that were only important and necessary for survival.

Dad mailed this picture home

Maybe being in the war and seeing life end abruptly, as it so often did, dad quickly realized how temporary life was and how you had to be ready to pick up and go, with few material goods, in the blink of an eye.

Some philosopher said that a strong
personality is one in which great contrasts
are present. I would have to say that
describes my dad. A hard worker, a devoted
man, sacrificial to a fault—and yet
sometimes hurting and embarrassing his
family through the things the disease of
alcoholism would cause him to do.

I can honestly say that at an early age I
knew that dad was distressed. I sensed that
there was something underlying it all, I
did know that he was a soldier before, but
I was too young to identify the source of
distress. I always tried to protect him and
still do today. Maybe this is to some
extent because; when I was young I
discovered many horrific Vietnam War
photographs that were scattered on the
floor of our attic. The images I saw were

of death. These were real images of real war that I will never forget. I can only imagine what it was like for him to see this happen before his own eyes in real life. Damn, no human being with feelings could act as if they never saw this happen. This would unquestionably change a person. Unbelievable!!

I realize now after my dad's death that he suffered from PTSD - Post-Traumatic Stress Disorder.

If you have ever been in a near accident—say, a car accident—and been calm during the time it was going on and then found yourself shaking afterward—you've had a taste of Post-Traumatic Stress Disorder. If you've ever lain awake at night, reliving a stressful argument you had with someone earlier in the day—unable to get it out of your head—you've had a taste of Post-Traumatic Stress Disorder. With PTSD, the memories come back, triggered by every day events or sometimes just rearing up when the mind is most vulnerable—like the time when you are trying to go to sleep or when you are off your guard. One Veteran fell apart whenever there was a loud noise or pop near him, suddenly transported back to the trauma of living on the edge of fear each moment in Vietnam, when a buddy might be downed forever by an unseen sniper in the jungle while going to do something as normal and everyday as going to go to the bathroom, or blown to smithereens right before your very eyes.

Some veterans lay awake at night, endlessly reliving the traumatic, violent scenes they went through, unable to shake them from their minds. The emotions are not always easy to sort out—people in war rarely behave with pure courage or pure cowardice, pure nobility or pure bestiality. They behave with a mixture of all those things, and the emotions surrounding their memories are often a mixture that is hard to sort out too—and hard to put to rest in peace.

In spite of the difficult circumstances in our life, I always loved my dad-an unconditional love. I wanted him to know how much I loved him, no matter what was going on. I remember long ago when I was young my mom asked all of the children who wanted to live with him when they got divorced. Maybe I felt sorry for him, but I was the one at the time who said I wanted to stay with him. Maybe it was because I knew the kind, generous, devoted heart that was within him and somehow I felt his suffering and pain. I now know his destructive behavior and chronic alcoholism were linked with his war experience. In many ways, I can't fault him. I don't think you can shake off a war experience and return to normal. It's something that stays with you, until you die. A Vietnam Veteran told me that it was unfortunate that my dad didn't stay in touch with his buddies after returning home. He thought most veterans did not at that time. He stated that reconnecting with a buddy could have helped close up a mental void that he was probably experiencing. I wish that I made this connection before he died and maybe I could have helped him cope with whatever he was suffering from.

Here's a little history of dad. He was born on July 8, 1950 in Antigo, Wisconsin, a beautiful farming and lumber community in the north woods. Later his family settled in a nearby town of Wabeno, Wisconsin. Dad was the second oldest of nine children.

Dad with his mother-my beautiful grandmother

Although his given name was Julius, he only went by Jerry, and no family or friends called him Julius. He was actually named after his great uncle Julius, which made some of the other family members upset because the great uncle was an alcoholic—a "stone cold alcoholic" as my great aunt stated. It's true that alcoholism is a family disease. I hear that when dad was young he went to meet his namesake who was living in a nursing home, but he was quickly run off. The great uncle didn't want anything to do with him. Maybe he was suffering from late-stage Alzheimer's?

During my adolescent years, dad did not live close to us kids due to his career as a union pipe fitter and welder from Chicago, Illinois. We often lost touch. His work kept him traveling city-to-city, and when I was eleven years old my mom moved all the kids to Florida to be near her side of the family. Not long after I remember our dad moving there too, but he had to leave shortly after due to his type of job and lack of work. I look back today and think, "At least he tried to move to be near us." I do remember feeling heartbroken when he left and I'm sure he felt the same way.

Trying to keep up with each other was difficult at times. My mom remarried to a man in the military and we transferred around a few times too. I would often call my grandma's or my aunt and uncle's house to get in touch with my dad. I would hear from dad's former girlfriend about how bad he was doing and that he was not only drinking a lot but also addicted to cocaine too. I didn't understand at the time what was going on fully, but I knew it wasn't good. The calls about him only upset me as a child and made me more concerned about his well-being. I felt hopeless in the situation. Really, what was a twelve year old going to do to help? Maybe she was trying to get us involved to try to stop him from using? The drug use was short-lived as he did receive treatment from the Veterans Rehab Center in Chicago in December 1988, which was a relief. I uncovered through medical records that dad self-admitted himself into the facility due to thoughts of suicide while under the influence. He said "Yeah I need some help", and reported depression. He stated "I think I want to kill myself, that's why I do it." He admitted to having episodes of shakes and visual hallucinations during withdrawals as he tried to stop on his own. He reported that he has been drinking alcohol for 20 years and this was his first time receiving detoxification and treatment. Dad told them that he and his girlfriend recently broke up which did not contribute to his decision to get help. He felt that his substance abuse problem was getting out of control and it was now affecting his employment. He reported that he was spending up to a thousand dollars a week on drugs. He told them that he had no contact with his ex-wife or his children in the past year, because they lived in Florida. He wanted to receive treatment at this point so; he participated in counseling, group therapy and attended educational activities during the 11 days of treatment. It is noted that he reached his maximum hospital benefits and also that he requested to be discharged so that he could return to work. Upon his release he was prescribed medication to treat alcoholism and he was advised to attend regular AA, Alcohol Anonymous group activities in his community. He was diagnosed with having alcohol dependencies along with a personality disorder NOS, not otherwise specified, which is a type of mental illness. This diagnosis is given when no other personality disorder fits the patient's symptoms. He must have been misdiagnosed? This should have been PTSD? Too many questions remain. If only my dad was still here!

During his stay in treatment he was asked about his military service history. He told them he was a Heavy Equipment Mechanic and that he saw combat while in the service. It was documented that he was never tested for Agent Orange exposure. I was surprised that there was no additional written information about his combat experience. Did they verbally ask more questions? Clearly there was some physiological trauma associated with his dependencies and war experience. He started drinking heavily while serving in Vietnam as he stated that he has been drinking for 20 years and he sought help from a Veterans facility. Why didn't he seek help at another hospital? Why did he choose a VA treatment center instead of another one closer to where he was living? He had his own health insurance! Why was he abusing drugs to hurt himself? I wrote a letter to the VA Hospital to ask only one question! I wanted to know if he was ever diagnosed with having PTSD – Post-Traumatic Stress Disorder. I wrote that my research regarding PTSD clearly defines what my dad was suffering from. Damn, I'm no doctor or psychiatrist and figured it out! I wanted

to know if PTSD was possibly documented

somewhere. In reply to my letter, I

received a copy of his medical records with

a cover letter stating that enclosed is a

copy of ALL archived records. I did not get

an answer to my specific question. I feel

like I'm left to sort through his medical

records, military documents and life to

make my own conclusion. I thought maybe in

1988, the hospital didn't assess patients

for PTSD like they do today. After

researching, I know that the VA was fully

aware of PTSD, but failed to correctly

diagnose him. PTSD was not a new diagnosis

at all. It was formally referenced as

having "Soldiers Heart" during the Civil

War, "Shell Shock" during WWI, "Combat

Fatigue" during WWII and "Stress Response

Syndrome" during the Vietnam War. I often wonder if they would have made the correct diagnoses if they could have offered effective treatment to help. I know that's something that I will never know. So sad!

Over the next few years I went to visit dad in Illinois. It was a memorable period because he had temporarily stopped drinking at that time. We spent quality time together doing normal family things, like eating dinner and watching movies. The visit was too short, but I had to return back home to Florida for school. I rode back with an uncle who was a truck driver. Before leaving the truck stop I asked dad to take a picture with me in a little photo booth nearby. He agreed, so we took a quick picture. I guess I wanted to keep that memory of us together that day. I remember riding down the highway, looking back at dad as we parted and wondered if that was going to be the last time I would see him alive. I often worried that he would pass away and thought that every time I saw him could be the last. It wasn't true this time, because I would see my dad again when I was eighteen years old, on my wedding day. It was a really nice day, seeing my dad and having him there on one of the most important days of my adult life. I recollect anticipating his arrival to the wedding ceremony. As I was getting ready I kept asking family if he was there yet. This was a wonderful moment in my life to have my dad walk me down the aisle. With all my siblings at the wedding we were able to take a family picture with all of us in it that day. We were able to capture him on video too. All of which I'm so grateful to have in my possession today. After the wedding, dad went to the bar across the street where we would meet up to celebrate later that day. It didn't matter to me where we went, as long as we could be in the company of my dad for a while.

Unfortunately, our time shared together was short because he went back to Illinois the following day to return to work. It was heart wrenching to see him leave again. My little sister was devastated to the point where she was chasing his car down the road crying for him not to leave. We felt joy with his presence and emptiness with his absence. It's amazing how precious time can be with a person that you love so much.

A few years passed since my wedding and my husband and I decided to go to Illinois to visit my dad. It was definitely a joyful time. I remember dad taking my uncle and husband to work with him early in the morning and none of them returned until late that evening. When they came back home, I asked my husband how much money he earned while working with my dad, only to discover that they never made it to work. They decided to bar-hop all day and night instead of working. My dad was grinning as he put his arms around me, telling me how much he loved me and asked me not to be mad. I wasn't mad at all. In fact, I was glad that my dad, uncle and husband got to spend time getting to know each other more.

Most of the time together was spent laughing, watching movies, exchanging stories and joking around. One night my dad's friend came over to hang out and at one point the friend started saying God wasn't real for whatever reason, but dad stopped him quickly, telling him that he knew that God was real, that he had made it through too much for there not to be a God. I found comfort in that—that my dad not only believed in God but was willing to stand up for what he believed in. I wonder now what all he had made it through—had God rescued my father from danger in Vietnam? I hear there are no atheists in foxholes—no atheists in war.

I would see dad again the next year due to my youngest brother being in a bad car accident that almost took his life at eighteen years old. As a back seat passenger, he was rear-ended by a nineteen-year-old drunk driver. The accident put my brother in a coma due to swelling of the brain. Fortunately, my brother made it through the tragic accident. I remember our dad calling us at the hospital from Wisconsin, lost for words and all upset and saying he went into the woods and was praying to God for his sons survival. I wonder why he went into the woods to talk to God to save his son. Was it that he spoke to God in the jungle to save himself while in Vietnam?

A few days later our dad arrived at the hospital in Florida, I was upset with him during this time because I could see he had been drinking a lot. Alcohol had been the cause of my brother's accident—the other driver was drunk. How could he even drink alcohol at a time like this? Of course, I ultimately forgave dad for his drinking but I was disappointed in him at the same time.

Why did he always have to drink to escape the pain of life?

Yet I now know that the pain of normal, everyday life can trigger memories in some war veterans that make it seem like they are back in the war zone, back in the place where your buddy can crumple up and die right next to you from a bullet or an explosion that could just as easily have taken you. I know that those chaotic memories of seemingly senseless, random violence, the sights and sounds of war are not easy to live with and that they can come back and create a need to drink alcohol when something bad or stressful happens in ordinary civilian life. It's like your war experience never leaves you.

Now I know too that alcoholism is a family disease—there is some genetic component to it that makes it run in the blood. That is one of the building-block ideas of Alcoholics Anonymous, the venerable program that has helped so many millions of people deal with the impact of this substance on their lives. Alcoholism is a disease—a disease that cannot be cured but that can be controlled through total abstinence and with the help of God. Thinking like this helps me to forgive my dad for some of the negative effects his drinking had on our family. So much of what he did he couldn't help, between the traumatic memories of Vietnam and the genetic tendency toward alcoholism.

That is why, for all the ups-and-downs of his life, I remember so much the generous, hard-working, loving and patriotic man he was—a man who bravely served his country and tried to do the best he knew how for his family —a man -my dad and my hero. I accept him for who he was, no matter what.

"For if you forgive others their trespasses, your heavenly Father will also forgive you, but if you do not forgive others their trespasses, neither will your Father forgive your trespasses." - Matthew 6:14-15

Chapter Two: In Country and Home Again

Quan-Loi area of Vietnam, near the "Thunder Road"

My dad was of German descent, with dark brown hair with little or no gray, even into his fifties, with dark brown eyes, an olive skin tone, and he was clean shaven most of the time. According to his military records, when he was seventeen years old, he was 5'7", weighing 160 pounds, with a muscular body. The combination of lean, fighting trim and the vulnerability in his young face touches me. The previous picture was taken when he was assigned to a camp in Quan-Loi. Quan-Loi was near an old Michelin rubber plantation and was also called LZ Andy over in Vietnam. It was near the village of Lai Khe, through which ran Highway 13 or the "Thunder Road" as they called it because of the constant mortar attacks against it. My dad's unit, the 557th, supported the 31st Combat Engineer Battalion, 20th Combat Engineer Brigade and the 168th Engineer Battalion. They worked on Thunder Road together. The area was a target for mortar attacks—a man who served with my dad says that not only were they hit with mortars almost every night, that, in fact, a truck took a direct hit right where dad was posing in the previous picture. They built and repaired roads, cleared areas for base camps and did many other support missions.

This is a picture of the 557th Engineer Company building a bypass road around the Song Be Fire Base. The mountain in the background is called Nui Ba Ra which is the sister mountain to Nui Ba Dinh (The Black Virgin Mountain). The Special Forces, Green

Berets had an "A" camp on the top of Nui Ba Ra, and the 557th Engineers had a fire base camp near the base of the mountain.

Unfortunately, the NVA had tunnels in the rock formation in the center and would fire at them every night as soon as the sun went down. Their tunnels were eventually exposed by throwing grenades into them and watching the smoke appear out of the other side of the mountain. Interestingly the U.S. Army would enter into the tunnels and find that the NVA stored ammunition there, and they actually had a hospital, mess facilities and sleeping quarters established in the center of the mountain.

Above is a picture of my dad's truck that
was blasted after he drove over a mine. It
makes me wonder if the explosion killed
anyone riding along, or caused dad to
receive a mild case of TBI - Traumatic
Brain Injury. It's common for soldiers to
ignore these types of injuries due to
chaotic events surrounding them. TBI would
explain his difficulties with suffering
with PTSD and the perpetual alcohol use. He
did later report to the VA that this blast

caused hearing loss. The areas where dad worked were known to be dangerous. There were several incidents reported of men being injured or losing their life due to detonating road mines, as well as causing extensive damage to their vehicles.

Highway 13 bisected the village of Lai Khe and was the main supply road running north and south, parallel to the Ho Chi Mihn Trail. By day, it belonged to the Americans; by night it was stealthily used (and attacked) by the Viet Cong or "Charlie". Not a pleasant or safe place to hang out, even if you did have an M-16 on you. My dad, like many soldiers, preferred the older M-14 to the M-16. Even though the M-16s were lighter and supposedly had better aim, M-16s had a tendency to jam.

Apparently Quan-Loi was an area with a lot of trees--rubber trees and other kinds. In that, it was pleasant, because shade was a luxury in Vietnam, although it did reach really cold temperatures at night. Shade could also be a protective cover at times. Sunlight exposed a soldier to danger.

The above photo is Highway 13 in the Michelin Rubber Plantation located on the

Cambodian border. Some of the 557th Engineers were doing the pioneer work on the road to prepare for the invasion of Cambodia. The road had not been used by heavy military traffic for over a year, as you can see the road appeared unused. The VC had blown up many of the culverts and left it in poor condition. The 557th Engineers saw NVA crossing the roads in groups of twos and threes. The Cambodia border was just a about two thousand yards away to the left.

Quan-Loi was a psychological black hole, in knowing that an ambush the previous year killed a lot of men. Thunder Road was still a dangerous, explosive place when dad was there, unsafe by day and absolutely treacherous by night. The village of Lai Khe was typical—you never knew if the

Vietnamese worker who performed some service for you that day—delivered your laundry, for instance—was a friend or an enemy. The Vietnamese had been fighting the French for a long time before America ever entered the war. To some of them, all Westerners were sometimes equated as being part of the old colonial powers they wanted to see out of their country. They did not understand that communist China and Soviet Russia were fighting a proxy war through the Vietcong to establish communist control in Asia and that the Americans were a safeguard against that. Many of them could not be trusted—a simple Vietnamese farmer you would pass along the Thunder Road by day might be planting a mine next to it by night, hoping to blow you to smithereens. A lot of soldiers talked later on about how not knowing who the enemy was and who was a friend—the fact that the battle lines weren't really clear—was part of the mentally and emotionally unhinging experience that was Vietnam.

Directly above is a photo showing two 10 ton tractors with 60 ton lowboy trailers and a ¾ ton in the background. The 557th Engineers are overnight somewhere, as you see the cot set up between the trucks. The guys would sleep underneath these big trucks at night because they provided some protection from incoming mortar and rocket fire. These big trucks were easy targets, and if one disabled on the roadway, it was difficult for following vehicles to get around them, so they were all trapped. Another 557 Engineer told me that at one time, my dad was his ¾ ton truck driver. Dad would drive him and others to job sites and base camps. He said that running convoys was dangerous duty and many truck drivers were killed while on convoy. The Viet Cong would attack a convoy that could not get around disabled vehicles due to surrounding rice patties. They would shoot a fuel tanker first using a rocket propelled grenade or any of the big trucks first. Then they would shoot up all of the vehicles that were trapped and stopped behind them. As a truck driver my dad would drive other unit guys to stand guard at designated areas near the parameters of their assigned base camp. Dad stayed with them to stand guard too. The purpose was to reinforce the line during ground attacks. Sometimes dad would man the M60 machine gun while the guys worked on their projects. Most of the time, the guys provided their own security. Dad also took care of the vehicles maintenance and repairs. I'm told that the Engineers were not considered infantry, but they got into a lot of shit, much more than other types of units. The engineers would be required to work at night sometimes to repair roadways, bridges, runways etc. and the Viet Cong would attack them as they worked, which resulted in deaths or serious injuries.

The guys were often separated to work on other projects and were assigned to different base camps, so they lost contact with each other. I read some reports about the engineers who were clearing jungles, and that their dozers would get damaged by the exploding mines or that the operators would get shot and killed by the Viet Cong. No wonder some of them drank to forget. Only they couldn't really forget, no matter how much liquor they drank. The memories stayed inside them until they received effective treatment to cope with the memories—something my dad never got. A man, a veteran—he probably thought he should be able to "handle it" himself. In some ways, he did. He was able to somehow maintain employment over the years. It was not until quite late in his life that his drinking actually completely interfered with his job. He started to get run off of jobs due to drinking. Losing a job is not an uncommon thing for anyone suffering from PTSD or alcoholism. Some vets have PTSD so badly, they cannot work. Sleepless nights and hair-trigger nerves make them unemployable. That was not the case for my dad, although his drinking, which I think was his main coping mechanism, it was clearly excessive. My brother, who occasionally worked with our dad, said at times dad would leave on his lunch break to drink alcohol and then return to work. Still, dad worked steadily before his last few years of his life.

Loving as he was, dad could have an irritable, angry side, especially when heavily under the influence. If dad was upset about something or with someone he could get really loud and say every curse word there was, as well as put up a good fight too. My uncle remembers how he never saw my dad lose a fight over the years. I'm sure he won most, but lost a few too. Dad could argue a point and stand up for what he believed in, that was for sure! I know he could be belligerent at times while drinking and he didn't want to hear anyone whining and complaining. He had zero tolerance listening to someone have a pity party. I remember when I was about eight years old; my mom locked our dad out of the house because he had been drinking so much. He was so upset that he kicked the kitchen door in and started yelling and throwing dishes randomly across the room. His disorderly conduct caused him to get arrested that night which happened before my own little eyes. In fear of his quick release my mom packed up all the kids in the van and quickly left the house. I recall waking up the next day still in the van. We had slept in the van overnight near our grade school. As hard as things were mom still returned home. Addiction specialist and alcohol addictive, say that being unable to understand that the negative consequences a person is racking up are directly due to the addiction is the sure sign of an addict. No matter what the consequences, the individual keeps using the substance of his or her choice—in my dad's case, alcohol. The addict can't see that their substance abuse is damaging their lives, or they are in denial that it is the substance causing all the trouble.

Sometimes they say it is other people who are the problem. My mom shouldn't have provoked him, he might say. Treatment programs for friends and relatives of alcoholics emphasize Three Cs: the friends or relatives didn't cause the addiction, they can't control it, but they can learn to cope with it and even live happy and stable lives whether the alcoholic is still drinking or not. They are not responsible for the alcoholic's drinking, but they are responsible for how they choose to respond to it. This kind of thinking empowers people who love someone who is addicted to something, be it alcohol or other drugs, to hang onto some sort of sanity in their lives.

I have chosen to respond to dad's drinking with forgiveness and love for the goodness in the man. No one on earth is faultless. I'm not making excuses for bad behavior, but only understanding. I hope others reading this story can forgive others or themselves for their addictions and struggles, past or present.

It's not that my dad never caused me direct humiliation with his drinking.

During the last year of his life, I was embarrassed while at a restaurant with him because he was so intoxicated. He got so loud that other customers were staring at us shaking their heads and even leaving their tables to get away from us. Quietly we sat there and finished our dinner—somehow without getting thrown out.

It was not unusual for family members to receive phone calls from the local bars at any given time. The bartenders would ask us

to pick dad up and take him home or
sometimes they would call upset and say if
we didn't come get him, then the police
were going to escort him out.

My husband told me that one time they
were almost thrown out of a poker
tournament because dad was so drunk that he
kept holding his cards off the table and
the dealer kept saying something to him
about it, but dad wouldn't listen.
Eventually, they had to leave and dad
passed out on the ride home which was
typical. Often his drinking resulted in
passing out anywhere at any time.

My husband and I were not the only ones
to suffer a bit of embarrassment because of
my dad's drinking. I remember one night
when dad was really intoxicated while
watching the movie *O Brother, Where Art*

Thou? with George Clooney. I watched the movie with him, he was singing along with all the songs, smiling and having a good old time. He loved, absolutely loved this movie. I can see why. It's a zany, picaresque adventure of three escaped convicts in the Deep South in the 1930s who somehow manage to get themselves in and out of all kinds of jams and wind up cutting a country music record together. I'm sure their crazy, escapee adventures in the vines and forests of the South reminded dad of the few zany good times he had in Nam. Some of the men who served with him have told me that they definitely had their good times together along with the bad and terrifying times. I'm told that my dad was a good guy and a good soldier who always made everyone laugh. They remember him as being dependable and a hard worker who always stayed out of trouble.

What was more, when I saw the movie, it reminded me of northern Wisconsin, with the small towns, surrounded by trees and rivers. It probably reminded dad too of when he was a child. Dad loved "*O Brother, Where Art Thou*?" so much that he asked my sister to take him to the store one night so he could buy the DVD. After they went to the store and got back into the car she noticed he hadn't bought the movie.

"Where's the movie, Dad?" she asked. "I thought you wanted it?" Dad laughed. "Right here!" he said, and pulled up his shirt. He had stolen the movie and stuck it under his shirt. My sister was so embarrassed that she vowed to never take him to the store again. To our dad, it was probably just all part of rule-breaking a high-jinx act for guys on the run for their lives to break up the tension. I heard that the guys in the Army had done some crazy things to stretch and break the rules just to feel like they are human beings—just to thumb their noses at the authorities who have so much say over their lives. I've read stories about soldiers playing catch with hand grenades.

I was told by a Vietnam veteran friend that the movie "The Deer Hunter" depicts the Vietnam soldier's experience with a lot of accuracy. In it, soldiers become injured playing Russian roulette with real rounds. Is it because the whole situation is so risky, taking more risks is like an antidote to the poison of constant fear? Maybe. In light of all that, swiping a video from a store seems pretty small and forgivable to me.

Another movie mentioned from my veteran friend was "Distant Thunder", featuring John Lithgow. He thought this movie was the most realist version of what it was like for a returning Vietnam Veteran. He even told me that he could never share that thought with his own children. It was too disturbing. The movie portrays how hard it was for our veterans to transition back into normal life again from serving in Vietnam. It reveals the ugly truth about that war and how society impacted their well-being by being so unsupported and hostile toward them. Watching this made me realize how difficult life was for my dad returning home and how brave he was to wake up each day.

I know excessive alcohol consumption can lead to periods of temporary memory loss or amnesia. I think my dad proved this one day. He filed a police report that someone was stealing his money out of his personal bank account. He even ordered a review of the bank surveillance to reveal the thief, only to discover he was the one withdrawing the money.

One time my dad and uncle decided to take a taxi ride out of town to play poker. When they arrived there, the place wasn't even open. That joy ride cost him over two hundred dollars. Looking back, I bet they still enjoyed the ride together drinking and telling stories along the way. I guess I understood my dad's relationship with alcohol at times because, to be honest, dad's drinking made some happy memories for me and other family members over the years. Most of the memories created were in an environment where alcohol was present, so I have to accept and cherish those moments we shared together. Good or bad, it was what it was. If he was still alive today, and I know what I know now, then I'd probably like to have a beer with him.

Sometimes our dad took us kids to the bar with him while he drank. It was different back then growing up; it wasn't unusual to have kids with you while being at a bar. I remember those times as enjoyable, listening to the jukebox play various music. I was given spending money to play games and eat as much junk food that I wanted. My dad had a lot of friends in the many different taverns and bars he frequented. It was something like a carnival or an adventure. Maybe he felt that way too at times?

Into his fifties, the drinking would take what Vietnam couldn't—my dad would die of health issues brought about by Post-Traumatic Stress Disorder and alcoholism.

He was only fifty-five years old.

Chapter Three: The Long Road Home

Veterans who served alongside my dad assure
me that there were peaceful and happy
moments in Vietnam too. This seems to be
one of those moments

"Serenity. Serenity in the midst of war." I

like this quote because you can see in the

picture of my father the white clouds in

the background. In Vietnam there was music—

and moments of peace--and there were

moments of beauty and serenity when white

clouds floated by.

Serenity is an important concept in Alcoholics Anonymous and its companion program for the friends and relatives of alcoholics, Al-Anon. Serenity is the goal—to remain serene even in the midst of the most trying and searing circumstances of life with an alcoholic—almost like serenity in the midst of warfare.

The Serenity Prayer is recited at the beginning and/or end of every Alcoholics Anonymous meeting for alcoholics and Al-Anon meeting for friends and relatives of alcoholics:

"God grant me the serenity to accept the things I cannot change

Courage to change the things I can

And the wisdom to know the difference."

The Serenity Prayer is a prayer of comfort that helps one to keep steering one's ship steadily even in a rolling sea. They say trying to fight the battle of someone else's alcoholism is one war you will always lose.

If I accept the things I cannot change, one thing I cannot change is the past. I cannot change the fact that my dad died with having a failing liver at the relatively young age of fifty-five years old, due to alcoholism, due to unresolved issues he could not leave back in Vietnam. I cannot change that, so I must accept it and the sadness and regret that comes with it.

Over the years, dad had lost some of his height and weight. He was about an inch shorter in height and less than 130 pounds, which he was shorter and thinner than the strapping young man who had volunteered to go to Vietnam.

He was a simple man whose attire consisted mainly of jeans, cowboy boots, and a pocket t-shirt. Occasionally he wore a button up shirt. He wore a variety of different hats, although he was most likely to be wearing a welder's hat. He smoked cigarettes heavily--mostly short, full flavor packs. He had only one tattoo on his upper arm--a heart with a dagger through it. I see from old photographs that he got the tattoo sometime in his teens. He had it before joining the Army in early 1968.

Before he lost his driver's license permanently due to having too many DUI's he would own motorcycles, older sporty cars, and in the '90s he was the proud owner of a black extended-cab Ford truck which had running lights across the top, which he carried his welding equipment in the back along with work tools. He was very knowledgeable when it came to automobile issues.

A people person, he was very outgoing and charming with the ladies, as I saw him many times in the bars flirting and laughing with the waitresses and lady bartenders.

He also loved being around his grandkids. I remember him sitting on the floor one day playing a toy piano, singing and smiling with the kids. A real memorable moment of sincere happiness!

The week my dad passed away, my cousin told me that dad called her father, my uncle, and said he didn't think he was going to make it up there to see him before he died. He had a feeling that his life was ending. He knew his health was declining and he knew what he was experiencing. I wish I had known, so things could have been different.

My dad is now missing out on the relationships he had with his grandkids, his children, other family and friends. Of course, we too are missing out on having him around. I wish I could have saved him from all of the pain he was suffering.

My husband told me about an unexpected conversation he had with dad regarding Vietnam. One night he was driving down the road with dad after having a few drinks together and dad told him that he saw some bad things while in Vietnam. He stated," Death of women and children", and my husband responded by stating, "war was ugly." Nothing else was said about it. It must have been tough to carry that kind of pain with you for over 35 years. Who could ever erase those horrid images or disturbing thoughts? Was that the first time in a long time that he tried to open up about his war experience?

True war is ugly, but our soldiers have a job to do, which they are trained or ordered to do. Soldiers should not be ashamed of protecting themselves or others in a war zone. They try to survive and serve our country the best way that they can and make the best decisions possible. Sometimes a soldier only has a second to make a life threatening choice.

My uncle told me that he asked dad if he ever killed anyone. He never responded to the question. I guess he wasn't comfortable talking about it?

Back in 1987, I went to New York City and I saw a memorial wall at Battery Park with the name Julius Weber listed. I told dad about what I saw and nothing else was said about it until, many-many years later. He called me out of the blue one night asking me if I really saw his name on the wall. I said that I was pretty sure that I did. He said he needed to know because the Army lost his records. After dads death I researched the park that I once visited and I discovered there was a Julius Weber listed on the wall but, it was a memorial for a World War II soldier.

After dad passed away, a bartender from the Illinois marina told me that dad was where he always wanted to be and that was to be with all of his children in Florida. She stated that he constantly talked about his kids with her and he was so proud of us.

I continue to ask myself if we helped him enough? Could we have done more to help him stop drinking?

"Lord, help me to accept the things I cannot change"—especially the past. My therapist told me that just loving him was enough. I can say proudly that my dad was the best man I ever knew, in the good and the difficult times. He suffered from a horrible disease that is famous for taking lives and destroying families. It is a testimony to his heart that through it all, we still cared about him and loved him with all of our hearts. He was just that kind of guy you had to love.

In 1997, while dad was living in Wabeno, Wisconsin and he got really sick with pneumonia. He was in the hospital for a couple of weeks. I felt really sad that none of us kids lived near him and we were unable to be there with him. I frequently called him while he was in the hospital. I stated that I heard he had been drinking heavily, and I knew that he would be gone soon and I hoped that he knew that I thought about him all the time. I told him that if he passed away a part of me would go too. I just hoped to see him again.

My grandmother saw him walking down stairs one day and noticed how scrawny his legs were getting. He was so thin; she sternly told him he was going to go see a doctor. My grandma then took him to the hospital, and he was admitted. If not for this firm action on her part, he may not have lived as long as he did.

Sadly, my grandmother soon passed away and dad took the news of her passing incredibly difficult. He was working out of town when he received the news of her death and he regretted that he didn't get to say goodbye to her. He coped with the loss of his mother by drinking bottles of vodka every day. She was the center of his world! He was in a severe depression at this time. A few months later, he entered another detox treatment center. This time he lost his driver's license. Then received his license back but, later lost it again and never got it back.

In July of 1998, my dad phoned me at about 2:30 a.m. He sounded unhappy. He said he just took a bath and had noticed how he

had aged a lot. He was forty eight years
old now, and he felt he missed out on a lot
of his kids' lives. He said he was walking
one day from a family cookout and saw a
little girl sitting in her yard playing
with some toy and a little kitten. The
kitten was lying on its back, letting the
sun hit its belly. He said it reminded him
of us kids long ago, and he realized how
much we'd all grown up and he missed so
much of our lives. He had a lot of regrets
about the way he was living his life and
that he wasn't there to watch us grow year
by year. He talked about how much he loved
my mom too. This call was very special to
me. The words were from a man who regretted
the choices he had made and those choices
divided him from his family. He was
completely sincere, and it meant a lot to

me to hear him express himself. Before we hung up, he said, "My, it feels so good to hear your voice, Julie" and told me he loved me. For some unknown reason, I wrote this conversation in my personal diary.

In July 2000, dad came to town for a visit with us kids. He was turning fifty years old. He stayed with me for a week or so in Mobile, Alabama. We went to Florida to celebrate his birthday with other family members. This was the first birthday I remember having with our dad. It was one of my favorite memories we shared. My sister worked at a restaurant and bar at the time, so we had a birthday party for him there. We had several family members from my mom's side there to celebrate. My siblings and I bought our dad a pocket watch that had "Dad" engraved on the front. He was so emotionally surprised when he opened that gift. You could tell that he was so touched. There was a live band playing, and dad and I danced together that night to "You've Lost that Loving Feeling", by The Righteous Brothers. Thankfully, we captured several photographs that night.

I didn't understand why at the time, but this visit was very meaningful. One of my brothers later told us that dad came to visit us because he had been informed that he was dying and only had about five years left to live. My dad was coming to reconnect with his kids? At this time, all of us were busy with our lives, but we certainly appreciated him coming to see us and we cherished the time together with him. After a couple of weeks, he went back up to Illinois where he was living at a marina with my uncle and traveling between jobs. My older brother was also working with my dad at that time.

July 8, 2000

I'm thankful he could experience the peace and contentment that are evident on his face in this photo.

Dad would call me only months later distraught and when I asked him what was wrong, he told me that someone stole his pocket watch. The pocket watch meant a lot to him and now it was gone. I'm sure it was difficult for him to tell me that it was stolen but, it was not his fault.

That next year, unexpectedly my dad came to visit me again in Alabama. I think it was in the year of 2001. I received a late night call, which was from dad who was heavily intoxicated and he said, "It's your dad, come pick me up!" He got a ride from one of my truck driving uncles and he was dropped off at a gas station about 30 miles away from where I lived. I went to pick him up and brought him home where he would stay a week or two. I remember the first night he was there I was lying in bed crying, feeling confused and upset. My husband hugged me trying to comfort me. I was really disappointed with my dad for drinking and he was being so loud on the phone with his ex-girlfriend. I know dad and his former girlfriend had a rocky relationship—on and off again over the years. He kept swearing and yelling on the phone for hours and hours, which kept me awake all night and I had to go to work the next morning. After the first night dad's drinking was at a minimum without causing any further issues.

One night after work my dad, a co-worker and I went to a Mexican restaurant and we ordered him a margarita. As we sat there and ate, he looked like he wasn't feeling very well. As soon as we walked outside he started vomiting. I recall him apologizing to me for getting sick. This should have been a real sign of a declining health. I remember driving home after work and seeing him watch through the window for me as I parked the car. I thought it was really nice that he was there waiting for me. We went on several walks together in my neighborhood and one day he asked me if I thought he could quit drinking. Knowing me, I'm sure I encouraged him and told him he could. Although this was an unexpected visit, this was an extraordinary one to look back on because; I feel he was trying to bond with me in a special way. Maybe it was because he knew that he was dying but, couldn't tell me? Soon after he left, he called me when he made it to Illinois and told me he was sleeping in a Walmart store parking lot in a sleeping bag. He was going to see about a job in the morning. I don't know why he told me this because; it hurt my heart knowing he was not only alone, and sleeping in a parking lot but appearing to be homeless too? I never thought of him to be completely homeless because he always had close relations with his family and friends. I thought he still had money? Why didn't he rent a hotel room? This was one of the many moments that I suffered deep inside for him. An indescribable pain!

Over the years, we would keep in touch. By the time dad came back to visit again it was 2004 and I now lived in Florida; it was obvious that dad was seriously ill. At times he would run outside of my house to vomit and I found blood stains on his pillow and around my toilet seat.

We went to a bar one night, and I remember singing karaoke. My dad and older brother got up and sang "I Love this Bar", by Toby Keith. I dedicated a song to dad that night "Nothing Compares to You", by Shanade O'Connor. I remember looking at our dad sitting at the bar alone and I decided to walk over to check on him. He looked at me with seriousness and said, "You know I love all my kids, then hesitated and stated, "but I know you love me the most." Then he asked me to leave him at the bar to sit alone. I know that all of his children loved him. As the night wore on, our dad started to stumble around a bit, so we all told him we needed to get home. My dad asked, "Why? What's going on?" and started looking around the room ready to fight. He must have been through this before because he understood what was happening. Especially, when the doorman approached us to ask him to leave! Dad started yelling obscene words and we quickly walked out of the bar with dad trying to take his jacket off, ready to fight. I finally talked dad into getting in the car and I took him home with me before all hell broke loose. When we returned home, I quickly went off to settle in bed and dad was lying on the couch. I was laying there quietly wondering if dad was going to be okay alone and feeling like something was going to happen. I remember in the silence asking dad if he wanted me to take him to my brother's house. He responded by asking, "Is that where I belong?" I don't remember what my reply was, but I felt like I hurt his feelings that night and my heart sunk.

They say there are two kinds of alcoholics—ones who get happy and ones who get angry. My dad was both—sometimes he got very happy while under the influence and sometimes he got very angry. When I was younger, I heard many stories about him being a bar room brawler who didn't take crap off anyone. My uncle told me that one night he was with dad at the bar and there was a guy sitting next to them who upset my dad by the way he was talking and acting. A few minutes later the guy was knocked out on the floor. Dad never even got off his bar stool. He just continued to drink as if nothing happened. Another story I heard was that dad walked into a bar where some guy was flashing a gun around. The bartender whispered to tell dad that someone had a gun in the bar. Dad jumped up quickly and asked loudly, "Who has a gun"? He then walked over toward the guy and took the gun away. Of course, he beat the man up and threw him out of the bar. Maybe it was from serving in Vietnam that my dad spent the rest of his life unwilling to take any "crap" off of anyone. He'd been there, done his time, and he didn't have to be afraid of anyone. At times, I think he thought he was bulletproof.

I've heard that many of dad's earlier fights in the 70's were caused when he overheard anyone talking out of sorts about the Vietnam War. This would cause an immediately uproar.

In 2004, my husband told me that dad opened up to him one night and told him that he didn't have much time left and that he was seriously ill. My dad did not open up with me directly about his health issues at that time but, my husband would often tell me to spend quality time with my dad.

Dad returned back to Illinois and over the next few months we would learn more about his illness. I received one of many calls from a local bartender who really cared about my dad's well-being. She would tell me stories of finding him passed out in the bar parking lot. She warned us that if we didn't come get him, he would die on a bar stool. The bartender recalled dad saying that he didn't care about dying and that if it was his time to go, so it was, and then he'd raise his drink and shout cheerfully, "Let's drink to that!" This behavior really upset the bartender and she often would go home after work and cry, because it was so sad and she hated seeing him so sick and vomiting blood and just being so careless.

Everyone seemed to be concerned about my dad's health except for my dad himself. He accepted the fact that he was dying and did not want any medical help. I know at times he was drinking even more to end his life earlier, trying to hurry it up.

"The LORD is close to the brokenhearted and saves those who are crushed in spirit."

Psalm 34:18

The marina where dad hung out and lived for eight years. In spite of its sign "Four Star Marina—Where the Fun Begins" the fun was starting to end for my dad.

The marina was a beautiful place right along the Illinois River in Ottawa, Illinois. It was a hot spot for some of the residents. The above photograph was taken in October 2005 following my father's death. We traveled through there to pick up my uncle so he could attend the funeral of his brother, my dad. This was the place where dad called home off and on for almost eight years. I understood why my dad enjoyed this place so much over the years. It was a place where he and my uncle lived together between jobs. The bar was walking distance to their travel trailer, and the people who lived there looked out for one another. My dad had a lot of friends and often had family members visit him there.

Unfortunately, his party never seemed to end. One night in August 2004, a paramedic stopped by to check my dad's vitals and said he needed to get to the hospital immediately, but dad refused. My uncle said dad looked nine months pregnant and needed medical help. Finally, dad gave in and went to the local hospital where they drained some of the excess fluid from his stomach. After four days he was transferred to a Veterans hospital in Chicago where he would stay for a week. I spoke with the hospital administrator to ask if dad's condition was so severe that I needed to go there to be with him. The response I received convinced me that I did not need to go right then, but I should persuade him to move to Florida to be with his children and receive additional medical help in order to prolong his life.

I stayed in touch with dad during his stay in the hospital. He asked me if he came to Florida would I promise to be there to hold his hand in the end. I promised him that I would, but he continued to refuse to move by us and said he was not living off of his kids. My dad would say that he wasn't going to live in a nursing home either. He was an independent person who took care of himself. I told him that he would not live off his kids and he could take an early retirement from the pipefitters union and receive social security payments.

According to dad's medical records at that time, he had generalized weakness, appetite loss, weight loss, he was malnourished, had jaundiced skin, lungs that were short of breath, other respiratory issues, a chronic cough, pale skin, swollen ankles, and abdominal fluids but his vital signs were stable. It was noted that he was at risk for withdrawal and that he would need to be evaluated for an alcohol rehab program. It was also noted that most of his problems were probably related to his alcohol use.

Dad informed the doctor that he ultimately wanted to move to Florida upon discharge, where he could live with non-drinking family members and get away from the drinking scene at the marina where he lived. A nutritionist came to consult with him regarding his diet and it was noted that dad reported he lived with his brother and he did most of the "cooking", eating two meals a day with six to eight cans of beer. Meals consisted of canned soup and sandwiches ("Ham, bologna--we mix it up," he told them) and that his brother worked whenever he-my dad had a job. His brother was also in the pipefitters union and they worked together most of the time.

Dad was diagnosed as having cirrhosis of the liver along with other serious health conditions. Some recommendations made were that he needed an evaluation for his esophageal varices, lung lesions, liver problems and more. Dad was informed about the severity of his illness and he specified his status as a DNR/DNI--do not resuscitate. He was counseled to stop drinking and to take all his medicines and vitamins as prescribed and to move to Florida with his children and a new scene.

After being released from the hospital, he returned to the marina and continued drinking heavily. The bartender would continue to call me with concern, stating again that he was going to die on a bar stool if we didn't come get him.

After a month or so he decided to move to Florida and transfer his medical care. His initial arrangement would be to stay at my mom's house with his son, who was living there. Mom was not living home at the time because she was an over the road truck driver. I remember my brother and me taking dad to his first doctor appointment. Of course our dad drank the night before, so he was still a bit intoxicated. I will never forget the doctor coming back with our dad after the endoscopy. I asked the doctor in front of dad how long he had to live and the doctor looked at my dad sternly and said he would be gone before his next birthday, which was in about nine months. My brother and I asked to see the doctor privately and we explained that we were taking care of our dad and he had just moved here to be with us. The doctor said rudely, "Send him back to where he came from! I've seen his kind before, and he will never change. He will just cause problems in our family and likely burn a

house down while he's at it." My dad
apparently pissed off this doctor!

My brother and I were stunned at his
response, but I think it gave us more
strength to vow not to give up on our dad.
Maybe dad had already given up, but we were
not going to give up on him. Shortly after
that doctor visit, our dad was to follow up
with another appointment to receive an
official letter stating his terminal
illness: cirrhosis of the liver. We then
went to the Social Security office to apply
for benefits and requested early retirement
from the union. Thankfully, he didn't have
to wait long before his benefits began.

Dad moved out of my mom's to live in a
cottage-style apartment on his own. It was
a nice space for him but it was not in a
recommended area of town. One night dad met

up with some strange guy who was living next door and dad took him to eat and have drinks at a nearby restaurant. After dinner they were walking back to the cottage when all of a sudden this guy started to beat on my defenseless-intoxicated dad to steal his money from him. I received a call from the police, asking me to assist dad because he was refusing to go to the hospital, even though he really needed to go. My brothers and husband quickly ran to be with my dad to comfort him and help clean him up. The crazy lunatic was immediately apprehended and taken to jail where he belonged. Sadly, I recall my dad not wanting to press charges. That was the kind heart he had. Dad was always kind to strangers and helped anyone in need. The family had warned him several times to keep his money hidden or he would get robbed. He carried a lot of money with him at times. Well, this fear became a reality. Thankfully, after this tragic event, he bought a 30-foot travel trailer. He moved the trailer onto my mom's property, which was a perfect arrangement for his well-being.

Things seemed to go well for a while and at my dad's next doctor visit, he was able to surprise the doctor. When the doctor asked him how much he had to drink, he replied, "Not a drop!" The doctor was pleasantly surprised at this response, since weeks before he said dad would never quit. However, this dry spell would soon end. Unfortunately!

My husband, dad and I went to watch our first movie together at a theater: "Ray," the extraordinary life story of Ray

Charles, which was a bit intense with the realistic drug abuse and horrific loss of his brother scenes. On our drive home after the movie, Dad asked to be dropped off at a bar. I quickly said, "Dad" with disappointment in my voice, but he said that he needed a drink. I was proud of him for stopping, then disappointed in him for starting up again. I just knew that it would be some time, maybe never, before he would be able to stop drinking. I still loved him, but it was hard to see him start up again. I couldn't stop loving him because he was drinking.

Chapter Four: Downward Slide

I've learned that part of the soldier's mission in Vietnam spilled over into Cambodia because the Vietcong would slip over the border for sanctuary there. In spring of 1970, when dad was in the area, U.S. Army Engineers were asked to go into Cambodia to support battling the Vietcong in their sanctuaries. The soldiers in Quan-Loi, where my dad was, supported these missions through road-building, repairing and construction. One veteran I correspond with says he and my dad worked together in Cambodia, a dangerous and difficult mission. Supplies were low there and the water was all malaria-infested. They could drink nothing but treated water, and it was always tepid or hot, never cold.

After suffering so many privations in such distant foreign lands, when the soldiers came home, they were mistreated by civilians because many people were against the war. So they not only came out of the difficult situation of war, facing a terrible enemy and putting their lives on the line every day and night. They came home and were spat upon, told off, called "baby killers" and treated as if they had done something shameful by answering the call of their country. I believe that some of the news media caused a lot of the delusional thoughts about the war, which caused an erroneous perception of what was really happening. Sadly, there were countless civilians killed during the war and it's a devastating fact that should not be forgotten. I've read reports that indicate that some civilians were defined as "an enemy"; because they were within free-fire zones or the civilians truly were "enemy soldiers" disguised wearing civilian clothing.

I understand that America had an immense amount of cowardly draft dodgers and their supporters rationalizing why they refused to serve their county. They caused riots and chaos to avoid serving our country and that's something a person will have to live with for the rest of their lives.

I learned that the military often made friends with the villagers who were orphaned by the Viet Cong. The soldiers regularly provided them with security and support including sharing candy and their own C-rations with them. The U.S. military personnel administered medical care for the villagers and I heard that the children were often the highlight of a soldier's time spent in Vietnam. They looked after the orphans and even built playgrounds with excess building materials, so they could play and enjoy themselves.

The 557th Engineers often aided in construction of wells for villages and taught the Vietnamese techniques to use it properly.

The U.S. Military would hire Vietnamese to help fill sandbags, cut grass, provide laundry and maid services, etc.

No matter how a person may feel about the Vietnam War, Americans did not do right by our returning veterans, and their chances of healing their psychological and emotional scars were decreased. Many of them already felt guilty, not necessarily about participating in the war, but guilty over things they had done or not done. Some of them were haunted by being unable to save buddies' lives and even felt guilty over having survived when so many others didn't. They had plenty of heavy burdens to bear without being blamed when they came home.

My own dad's homecoming from the war was unwelcoming from strangers but, supportive from his family. The family had a celebration at a local tavern, and the only people happy to see dad were the family members. Others in the tavern started making argumentative comments, saying my dad had no business in Vietnam, which was followed by an uproar and brawl. This was the thanks he received for serving our country. My great aunt says our soldiers were called idiots for serving in Vietnam or you were called a coward if you took off to hide from the draft, so you were damned if you went and damned if you didn't. My dad lost a childhood friend in Vietnam who was killed in action. His friend wasn't even there six months before he was killed.

Many of our Vietnam veterans returned home and weren't accepted back into their own families because they were so ashamed of them. A veteran told me that when he came home from Vietnam he and others were told they weren't allowed to join their local American Legion. A girlfriend of mine was told by her parents that she wasn't allowed to date a Vietnam Veteran. Some Vietnam veterans at that time were mistreated by veterans of other wars because the United States pulled out of the war in Vietnam, and the other veterans respected them less on that basis. They weren't thanked for their service as they arrived to airports; in fact they were stared down and avoided.

Even today, forty years later, we still have Vietnam Veterans who are suffering indescribable pain, physically, mentally, and emotionally. It is tragic!

However, I am glad to see that, no matter how people feel about the current wars, we have since learned to show respect to the men and women in uniform who have put themselves and on the line to suffer more than most of us ever could ever imagine.

This is Dad in uniform at a tourist spot.

I found this picture interesting because it was laminated. Makes me wonder if he carried this photo around with him while serving in Vietnam?

I remember, one day dad stated that he wished he could serve in the Iraq and Afghanistan war instead of sending our young men. Was he trying to protect the young soldiers from experiencing the hell that he went through? Most likely!

According to a survey done by the Washington Post, one-fifth of all the men and women who return from Iraq and Afghanistan have psychological problems from the stress they have endured. Some inflict injury upon themselves. The U.S. Army did not start keeping statistics about soldiers inflicting injuries upon themselves, even committing suicide, before 1980, but if you read soldiers' accounts of their time in Vietnam, it was known to happen. It was not totally uncommon.

Frankly, dad's drinking in the last years of his life was like suicide. The years were like a slow suicide, and the last few years, I often thought he was deliberately drinking more liquor to end his life.

Studies have determined that suicide risk is higher with those suffering with PTSD due to ineffective coping methods and not expressing their feelings. Disturbing thoughts of war can become overwhelming for veterans to manage and cause extreme grief and suicidal idealization.

Modern brain research coming out of Israel, using MRI techniques on the brain, shows that some people respond more strongly to stress than others do. I wonder if it was not the more sensitive types who suffered the most from Post-Traumatic Stress Disorder, like my dad. He was a loving person. I can understand why he felt he had to drink to forget his experiences in one of the most traumatic wars America has ever fought. Many alcoholics drink without having experienced a war, because they are sensitive people. A friend of mine who is in Al-Anon, the companion program of Alcoholics Anonymous for friends and family members of alcoholics, said, "I never met an alcoholic I didn't like." They are usually charming and sensitive people who have a hard time coping with this difficult world of ours. I think dad was one of those sensitive people who had to blunt the ugliness of war and life with alcohol.

One of the highlights of dad's life during his last year was the weekly Friday night poker game "Texas Hold 'em." This was a weekly game of poker which dad always looked forward to. He was known to say "I'm all in," whether he had a good hand or not. It may of have been his great enthusiasm for the game, but over betting happened more often the more he drank. My husband, brothers, in-laws and others would play with him. My husband told my dad he was going to place a royal flush in his hands when he passed away, and dad would jokingly play along with him.

Christmas was coming soon and my uncle was moving down to be with my dad. My uncle and dad were not only brothers but the best of friends too. They lived and worked together for about eight years in Ottawa, Illinois at the Four Star Marina, and they were constant drinking and working companions. My uncle liked to drink Jack Daniels whiskey, and my dad liked Jim Beam

whiskey. Often I said they were the odd
couple or the blind leading the blind.

I have a favorite moment after my uncle
arrived that stays fresh in my memory. I
went to visit the two of them and when I
walked in dad's house they were sitting on
the couch with their arms around each
other's shoulder and neck, tapping their
feet and singing country music. Dad's
little Christmas tree lights lit up the
dark room. To be honest, they were
intoxicated but they were so happy to be
with each other. I don't think either of
them had a care in the world at that
moment.

Liquor could make dad seem so happy at
times, but I had mixed feelings about it,
since he was now dying. I didn't mind if he
drank beer to enjoy himself, but it was

when he drank excessively, and clearly, my

dad had gone that route too many times.

Still, we had great times together.

I went to visit them Christmas night to

exchange presents and hang out.

Dad always loved music and having a good
time. I'm sure he enjoyed the USO shows
with Bob Hope when they came to his area of
Vietnam

We played some old country music and sang

along to a variety of songs and laughed

together. Dad would play music by Dwight
Yoakam, George Jones, Johnny Cash and other
great country singers, but his favorite at
the time was any Merle Haggard song. I
remember one Vietnam War era song from 1970
titled *"The Fightin' Side of Me"*. What a
great American Merle Haggard is for
honoring our men and women during this
time!

I played Texas Hold'em one night with dad
and other family. We had a great time, an
evening full of laughter, yet I remember
dad was so intoxicated that he never
remembered me playing with them. We could
have such great times together, with his
alcohol included, but it just kept getting
out of control.

Since dad's drinking was continuing, our
family was getting increasingly concerned

with his health. We asked him to slow down because we didn't want to lose him. Dad wasn't as concerned as we were which made matters tougher. I used to ask him, "What's the big party about Dad?" I just couldn't understand the heavy drinking, especially when he knew that he was dying. I thought with him coming to stay with the family in Florida that he was going to seek additional medical treatment and try to sustain his life. Instead he was drinking as heavily as ever, maybe more so. I was really frustrated with his addiction and carelessness. At times, I didn't want him living near us anymore. I couldn't stand watching him go downhill. I was hopeless.

One time I went to visit dad while he was on one of his drinking binges, and he was vomiting blood. It looked like a 2 liter

bottle of coke gushing out of his mouth.
This scared the hell out of me! I just knew
he was going to die. I remember dad trying
to grab for my hand, telling me he loved
me, but he continued to drink his whiskey.
I was so upset with him and his condition
and his unwillingness to get medical help
that I quickly left upset. I even
apologized to my uncle before I took off. I
apologized for him having to sit there and
watch my dad kill himself. I know my uncle
certainly did not know what to do at this
point either. Ultimately, soon after I left
I think my uncle convinced him to go to the
hospital. When I arrived at the hospital, I
went in the room to see him. He was lying
there about three sheets to the wind. I
remember standing out in the hallway as he
was being wheeled away in his hospital bed

to get an X-ray. He was looking back at me, yelling, "Come with me, Julie," "Come with me" smiling and chitchatting, not taking this situation serious as his butt was showing through the hospital robe as he rolled away. I was a bit embarrassed, as hospital workers were staring at me and him, which now I do find it to be a bit funny. He was soon released from the hospital because he refused treatment again. I personally found that some medical professionals have little patience working with addicts. I believe that they limit their assistance with people who don't help themselves. I think that in my dad's case and for many others suffering from addiction, the truth is that they can't help themselves. Also, it's hard to help people who can't help themselves, especially ones with PTSD. People think they should just be able to shake or lift themselves out of it, but they can't.

I hear that some soldiers came back from Vietnam and say the rest of their lives were just gravy from then on. Having seen what they'd seen and done what they'd done, they never quite blended into the conformity of everyday civilian life again. War changes you! I don't think you care quite as much what other people think of you once you have been in a foreign country and seen the world a bit, and especially when you've known real danger, day in and day out. What can the opinions of some neighbors or some hospital personnel matter when you've faced death day after day for years on end? That can be a good thing or a bad thing. It can make you independent and fearless, or it can make you feel like you have nothing to lose any more.

The liquor really had a hold on dad by this time. One day I was at work and he called me to say that my uncle was there with him to help him die. What would make him say this to me? I got so upset that I left work to go to him. On my way, I stopped at the local paramedic's station and asked if they would go check on my dad. I explained that he was drinking himself to death but, the paramedic stated that my dad had the right to die if he chose to. This was confusing for me. I didn't understand why someone couldn't help my dad even if he wasn't helping himself. Weren't paramedics there to save and rescue people—even if it meant saving them from themselves? I even sought help by calling an 800 self-help hotline.

Dad was so far gone at this time that even his hygiene was suffering during his whiskey binges. I was so worried about him that I called local law enforcement and asked them to come and check up on my dad.

The officer came out and spoke with dad, but he said he wasn't a threat to anyone else and he did not have the power to make him go to the doctor. I was confused about all of this. It seemed like dad's actions against himself should be illegal—he was hurting himself so much with all this. I felt as if society didn't care one bit about my dad, whether he lived or died. I thought I needed to take additional steps. I went to the local bar he frequented and asked them not to serve him any hard liquor anymore. I told them my dad was dying and the liquor would kill him. The bartenders tried to be responsive and helpful. This seemed to work better than approaching medical personnel and police officers, because several times my dad called me from the bar and asked me to intervene with the bartender to grant them permission to serve him liquor. Of course, I said, "no" and told him that "I loved him" and hung up the phone many times.

Al-Anon, a program for families and friends of alcoholics, tell you that you didn't cause the drinking problem, you can't cure it, and you can't control it. In fact, they urge you not to intervene in the natural consequences of someone else's drinking. You shouldn't bail them out of jail, try to hide liquor from them in the house, try to coerce or force them or bribe them or yell at them to stop drinking. They say none of that will work. Eventually, the person has to feel the consequences of his or her own drinking, "hit bottom" and decide to change. Some people do hit bottom and change, but that is not guaranteed. By this time my dad was too far gone just to let the consequences fall where they might.

I was trying to save his life, but it was futile. It was too late for my dad by that time? I just never gave up doing whatever I could do to help.

I remember one night when I went to visit dad and he was soaking wet, cold, shivering a bit, and appeared frightened. He told me that he was walking home from the bar and got lost and fell into a pool of water, most likely a ditch along the road. I guess he thought he was going to drown. If he was drunk before he fell into the water, he appeared sober now. I didn't know what to say, but I was glad he was home safe.

Another terrifying time was when my brother was driving down the street at night and saw our dad passed out on the side of the road. My brother couldn't believe what he was seeing with his own eyes. He even thought that dad done it deliberately, because it was so unreal. He had numerous falls, which caused minor injuries. I often wondered how he stayed alive as long as he did. I'm sure my dad wondered the same thing at times.

As strange as those incidents were, there was a stranger one yet. My brother's girlfriend was driving dad down the road one day, and when she stopped he got out of the car and went and hid behind a bush. She got out of the car and went over to him, and he told her to get away--that it wasn't safe. He was digging in the dirt, making a hole. I am pretty certain he was having a flashback of Vietnam. No other explanation makes sense. Soldiers often dug holes to hide in if they couldn't find natural protection from gunfire elsewhere.

Soldiers often return to scenes of war in their memories

Sometimes I would ask him, with love, to stop drinking. He would tell me I didn't understand. I would tell him if he loved us and wanted to live longer, he would quit. In fact, that is not the truth, as I now know. Alcoholics drink in spite of how much they may love the people around them. In some ways, even though it affects people personally, it is not a personal thing. It is a real disease. You wouldn't tell someone to quit having some type of cancer or that if they loved you they wouldn't have diabetes. The alcohol had a hold of my dad and it was controlling his life. No one in our family was equipped with the knowledge necessary to help him or ourselves.

Throughout the years there were good times between dad and me. We frequently talked over the phone. We could talk for hours and hours. We would exchange advice and talk about the normal daily life regarding work, home, grandkids, and normal family conversations etc. He would help me out with special projects around the house and work on my car when needed. In fact, he was always willing to offer help with anyone who needed it. We watched movies and went shopping together. He loved to cook and was not a bad one either. He tried to teach me how to cook northern beans one day and I totally messed them up. I knew they tasted awful but, he didn't complain and ate them anyway. We shared quality time together especially when he wasn't drinking heavily. He was a good person who genuinely cared about his family. He always asked everyone if they were doing okay or asked if they needed anything. He was a proud dad who put each of his kids on a pedestal. Each of the children had their own special relationship with him. I remember dad telling me that he missed waking up at night and having all the kids in his bed.

At times he said he awoke wet with pee and it didn't matter. He loved having all of us together. My mom asked dad one day why he never married again and he said, "Once you had the best, there ain't no other." Another time he told her "you know you're the only girl I ever loved". He apologized to her about their earlier life together and told her that he could never take back what he did.

Under all the pain he was still the light of the whole family. He was our maverick, a great friend, the tough guy, someone who stood tall, made everyone laugh, and cry at

times. He was a great storyteller and was

never afraid to have fun. He was so full of

life and love. Anyone who knew him couldn't

help but love him. He was a true genuine

person who had the power to make others

feel special and loved. He was the best!!

I could always tell when he was drinking

hard liquor because he would call me and

ask, "Who loves you more than I do?" then pause and say "Don't nobody, baby," or he would start to make whistle-like sounds with his mouth. It was a dead giveaway that he was drinking his liquor. He used to ask me if I was trying to save him. Maybe!

Eventually, my mom told dad if he didn't stop bringing the liquor to his house that he would have to leave her property. We tried anything we could, to try to eliminate the hard liquor because we knew that it was killing dad faster. This caused him to sneak and hide the whiskey then. It was so painful for the family to accept. My sister says dad used to pull out small whiskey bottles from his boots to drink. He hid his liquor there in an attempt to hide it from mom.

My dad went through short periods away from alcohol and went to his regular doctor visits, mainly at the local Veterans Administration clinic. I later found out, that he refused their offer of counseling services. I remember in the spring of 2005, he was really weak and unable to get around. I took dad and my uncle to the beach, just trying to get them out of the house, but soon my uncle asked me to take them home. My uncle was literally holding dad up to bring him back to the car. Not because of drinking too much, but because he was so ill. I should have known he was too sick to go, especially since my uncle had to assist in dressing him that day. I quickly brought them back home so he could rest.

In June 2005, dad went on another bad
drinking binge, and I thought for sure this
was it and he was going to die. His arms
were bruised and his stomach was swollen
again. My mom even returned home from her
trucking job thinking this was it and was
preparing to care for him until he passed.
We took dad to the emergency room to get
checked out. My mom and I left the room for
a few minutes, so we didn't get to hear
everything that was said by the doctor.
When we returned to the room, we heard the
doctor tell dad that the fluid in his
stomach was okay and that his lung cancer
was in remission. This was the first time
we heard a doctor say anything about lung
cancer. Maybe the Agent Orange exposure
caused some of his health issues? Again to
our surprise, he was released from the

hospital. My mom and I think that while we were out of the room, dad asked to be released. I guess, they had to follow the patient's wishes, even if his wishes weren't helping him. I personally started attending therapy sessions after this incident, as I realized I needed some coping skills for what lay ahead. I also started going to church on a regular basis to gain some spiritual guidance and relief. I was in need of peace and comfort during this difficult time in my life. I would pray constantly for my dad, and my therapist gave me the best advice: she said to just love him. She knew I was trying to change him to save him and that I would not be able to do so. My dad had to make the change and decide to live a healthier life without alcohol. No one could do it for him. She told me that I was being the parent and my dad was supposed to be the parent. As his family, we were "powerless over alcohol" and needed to be "restored to sanity".

Over the next few weeks, dad quit the hard liquor and things seemed a little better. We spent our first Father's Day with him as a family, which was wonderful. Unfortunately, he was laid up ill that whole day, but he was home and sober.

We had a memorable Fourth of July with him. Our family went to a local pier to watch the fireworks display. It was an amazing display, with patriotic music playing in the background. I was standing there with my arm around dad's shoulder watching the 20 minute fireworks display. I told him he was my hero and thanked him for serving in the Army. He looked at me and smiled as he stood proud during the national anthem playing in the background. I remember thinking to myself that this could be his last 4th of July. This certainly was a very special time together and one I will treasure forever. My brother and sister were there with us too. To this day, I try going to the same place to watch the display as it brings me comfort to remember that wonderful time with my dad.

Fourth of July 2005

Chapter Five: "Fifty-five and Still Alive"

Dad's birthday was only four days away on July 8th. I remember a conversation with him. He said, "Well, it looks like I'm going to be making my next birthday." He was so proud of the fact he was going to make it to his birthday despite what the doctor told him only 9 months ago. My uncle and he came up with a rhyme: "I'm fifty-five and still alive!"

We celebrated his 55th birthday at my house like he wanted, and I had my sister in-law decorate his cake with poker chips with the royal flush laid across the top of the cake. We had a wonderful time together celebrating his birthday. I videotaped our dad as my sister in-law brought him his cake with the candles burning. I said, "Dad, look at the royal flush on your cake!" Dad looked at everyone and said, "I have a royal flush. I have all of you guys." Our family then sang "Happy Birthday", and he was looking around at all of us and we were finished singing, but he paused, staring at the candles. I yelled, "We love you, Dad!" and he looked up at me and smiled. My older brother said, "Dad,

make a wish and blow out your candles."
Before our dad blew his candles out he
said, looking at us, "I wish everybody all
the happiness that they can get out of this
life."

It was just like him to wish something
for someone else. He could be such a joy,
regardless of the difficult times we had.
He was such a kindhearted person who put
others first, even when the alcohol was in
control. He used to bring home strangers
for a few days and tell us they were
destitute and in need. Soon he'd have to
run them off as they were spending or
stealing his money, but the generous
impulse was there. He was such a giver that
he'd forget he needed his money to last
throughout the month. He had a lot of pride
and didn't like to take from anyone. I

don't think he owed any financial debts to anyone when he passed. He had a burial policy to cover all of his expenses and even had a small life insurance policy still payable to my mom after 20 years of being divorce. I could count on dad if I needed anything--even just a good conversation. He was not a judgmental person and a great listener. He was easy-going, easy to talk with.

Even though dad never complained about being sick, his doctor ordered hospice so someone could monitor his vital signs and care for him when he worsened. Dad agreed to let hospice come in and set up a bed for him, and he was actually happy to receive their service, which was really a milestone for my dad. Soon after setting up the hospice, his insurance company put a stop to the use of their service due to the cost. Dad was disappointed, when Hospice came and took his hospital bed back. His doctor substituted a home health nurse, whose tenure with him was very brief. Dad turned down her assistance immediately. He told me when the old nurse came in his house; she asked if he wanted her to give him a bath. He said that he wasn't going to have an old woman give him a bath that he could take care of himself! He told her to leave and she stayed, so my uncle and he left in a taxi. Apparently, he left some candles going in the house because the puzzled, concerned nurse called me and told me he had taken off in a taxi and she was blowing out his candles because he was going to burn his house down. That was the first and last time she came.

I went to visit dad that same day to check on him, and he was sober and his discolored arms were clearing up and he seemed to be doing well. I told him that the Lord was taking care of him, which he didn't deny.

Sometimes my mom and I talked to dad about God. At one point he told us that he had done too much bad in his life to be forgiven. Mom and I told him that God would forgive him for anything if he just asked for forgiveness. There are many scriptures in the bible that teach the importance of forgiving others and ourselves. My dad said he had his own preacher and showed us something he received from an evangelist from television. I remember telling him that he was taking the right steps towards a relationship with God. This was astonishing to me, that he had contacted an evangelist from television. Today that talk gives me comfort.

"If we confess our sins, he is faithful and just to forgive us our sins, and to cleanse us from all unrighteousness." - 1 John 1:9

Over the next month or so, my uncle moved back to Illinois and my sister decided that she would move in with dad in order to try and help him. My sister never really had a chance to develop a father- daughter relationship being that she was only about three years old when our parents divorced. My sister knew him the least of all the kids. One time she went to visit him when she was about 12 years old, but quickly returned back home brokenhearted due to his obsessive drinking and absence.

My mom warned dad from the start that it wasn't a good idea for them to live together, but she let our dad make his own decision. Through many conversations later about it, I gathered that he wasn't really happy with the arrangement anymore. Dad became very aggravated one night when he was playing poker. His behavior indicated that he was taking out his personal anger toward the poker players. He was clearly unhappy about his new living arrangement. My sister wasn't home but he had a house full of people over playing cards and drinking. At one point, he started yelling and cursing at everyone to get the hell out of his house--that it was his house.

I remember going inside his house one day, and he only had a little portion of the room left to sleep in because my sister had moved so much of her stuff in there, which our dad allowed her to do and later regretted it. Anyway, our dad was now trying to make arrangements to move back up north to Illinois to be with my uncle. I know he missed his brother, for they were the best of buddies. Dad said he also wanted to spend time with his own dad (my grandpa) in Wisconsin. I remember telling dad that I wished I could take him up there to visit. My dad said he'd love that. I didn't get a chance to take him, which I now regret deeply.

It was the end of September 2005 when dad was leaving to go be with my uncle up north. Unfortunately, dad and my sister had a severe falling out. Dad was heavily intoxicated one night and got really upset, and he decided to call the police to have my sister removed from his house. He wanted her to move out of his place. When the police came to check out the situation, my dad ended up exchanging words with the police and he was taken into custody for the night to detox. It was unusual for dad to disrespect an officer, so he had to be really upset. Right after that incident our dad refused to go back in his place with my sister. My mom offered to let him stay at her house, but he declined the offer. My sister said she was pissed that dad called the police on her and she was unwilling to let dad back into his place with her. He attempted to reclaim his place one night and beat on the door and windows telling her to let him back in his place. Still pissed off at him, she told him "no". He told her that he was her dad and to let him have his place back. She was so angry with him that she yelled at him calling dad by his first name Jerry. She told him that he was never a dad to her and she refused to open the door. She never spoke with him again after this incident. Sadly, it's well known that someone suffering with chronic alcoholism or PTSD can disrupt families and destroy relationships!

Dad was packed and ready to leave the next week to be with his brother. He purchased his plane ticket to leave on Thursday October 6th, 2005. Dad was quite disappointed about it all, basically pissed off, but he kept telling me that he loved all his kids no matter what. I told dad that in spite of the situation that he and my sister would be back to normal soon. My sister paid for a hotel room for our dad for a couple of nights, and then he kept paying for hotel stays instead of staying at my mom's house for the week. This was an extremely difficult time, with his living arrangements causing much heartache in the family. Our mom didn't want to get involved with my sister and dad's dispute about his place, she had already warned dad that it wouldn't be a good arrangement. She just knew it was not going to work out from the beginning. When I spoke to my mom about my sister staying in the house, she walked away, upset. We didn't know what to do at this point. Even though we were all struggling to come up with a solution to dad's situation, none of us could find a way around it all. My mom was kind enough, after being divorced from him over twenty years, to open her home and property to our terminally ill father. My mom has a really big heart and she would do anything for her children, or anything to help anyone, and even our dad who she still cared about. She just couldn't help much in this situation beyond making the offers that he refused.

I tried to comfort our dad the best I could during this difficult time. I picked him up Sunday morning on my way to church because we were going to a birthday party for an uncle on my mom's side afterward. I remember dropping him off near the local bar he frequented and asked him not to drink too much and he said he wouldn't. For the first time I went to the church altar specifically to pray for my dad. The preacher and I held hands and prayed together for him. After leaving the church, I went to pick dad up from the bar, and we left to go to my aunt and uncle's house. I told dad that the preacher and I prayed for him, and he said that was funny because he had some experience that he would tell me about later. He never did tell me about the experience related to my praying with the preacher. I certainly was proud of him for staying sober for the day, so we could have a great day together.

We had a nice time at the birthday party. Dad and I ate lunch together. I know he commented on how great my aunt's potato salad was and he went back for more. After the birthday celebration, I dropped him off at his hotel. My heart was crushed to take him to a hotel, but he did not want to go back to my mom's house. He was leaving on Thursday to fly out anyway, he said.

On Wednesday after work I wanted to go and see my dad since he was moving away the next day. This was one of the most inspiring visits together that I ever experienced in our life. I went to a local bar where I thought he might be and when I walked in, there he was, alone at one side of the bar, having a beer and cigarette. We were really happy to see each other. I knew that I needed to see him before he went out of town the next morning. I had my teenaged daughter in the car and dad asked the bartender if she could come in. I was looking at the bartender, shaking my head no, but the bartender said, "Yes". So I walked out and got her and on our way back in, dad was rushing out the door, thinking

I wasn't coming back. He quickly smiled as he held the door for us to come back in and he put his arm around me as we walked back to sit at the bar. A little while later, I gave my dad a "Sinners' Prayer" which is a prayer asking God to forgive us for our sins and accept that Jesus Christ is our personal savior and through him we have eternal life. I asked him to read it later and that I'd get it back again someday. He then put it in his wallet. My dad then said that he wished he could carry me in his pocket, and we smiled. As he put the prayer away in his pocket, he jokingly said, "I'm almost afraid to read it!" I felt it was time to settle some uncomfortable, but important things since he was moving away. We talked about him leaving and I thanked him for coming to stay with us. I asked him about his wishes after he passed away, asking if he was sure he wanted to be cremated and he said," Why sure I do." I asked him if he wanted me to keep his ashes, and he said he never really thought about it. My dad and my uncle always joked around about being cremated and sent down a river in Wisconsin. Dad always believed that after being cremated you were truly free, free to roam wherever you wanted to go. I told him that he still had a couple years left. I guess we were trying to give each other hope and comfort during this questionable time.

My dad told me that he had no regrets in his life. He said that with sincerity. As we sat together, he looked at me as he had a year earlier and said, "You know I love all my kids, but you love me the most and paused. You came to see me." Our eyes were glassy with tears at this point. Dad was blinking, joking that something was wrong with his eyes, as he smiled and turned away. I offered dad a ride back to his motel but, he declined. Shortly after our conversation we said our good-byes. After my daughter and I left, we drove to my dad's hotel room to leave him a note on his door. The note stated that I loved him and I would be praying for him.

Thursday morning I called and spoke to dad before mom picked him up to go to the airport. Of course, I told him how much I loved and would miss him. Mom took dad to the airport but, they arrived a little too late and the flight was not taking any more passengers. My dad had missed his flight. I was at work at the time when I received a message from my mom regarding him missing the flight. Somehow, it seemed this was an opportunity and it was meant to be. I called mom back to ask her to seek medical help for our dad through the courthouse and keep him here instead of having him move away to die. To my surprise, when I called her before I even mentioned it, my mom told me that she and my sister were going to the courthouse to request a Marchment Act, which is court-ordered involuntary treatment for anyone who is chemically addicted or addicted to alcohol. This option seemed to be the best choice because, left to his own devices, we feared dad would die when he moved away. I wanted our dad to live as long as he could, and I wanted to be there for him when he did take a turn for the worse. I promised him that I would hold his hand when he died, and that he wouldn't be alone.

Friday afternoon my dad was picked up by authorities from the local bar and taken in for detox, but that night he was released from them to go in the hospital due to excessive blood loss. I received a call that night from a doctor at the hospital informing me that dad was dying. I was confused, though. We knew he was terminal for quite some time. He had been in and out of the hospital several times in the past year, and I didn't think this time was any different from the others. The doctor told me that he was stable and being sent back to detox. This call disturbed me, but I thought we finally have real help for him. I put the situation in God's hands. I remember calling my mom about the conversation between the doctor and me. I was afraid that dad might die in detox. I recall the prayer I prayed that night, asking God to send his angels to my dad's side to save him.

As I awoke on Saturday morning, it was October 8, 2005, I recalled the doctor's comments which still disturbed me so; I called the doctor to ask how long she thought my dad had to live. Maybe we need to forget about this program? When I called the hospital, the operator asked for my dad's name and when I told him, he said that my dad was in ICU. I said, "ICU? What do you mean?" and he transferred me to the nurses' station in the ICU—Intensive Care Unit. I gave the phone to my husband as I started to get dressed in a hurry to go be with my dad. My husband asked about his medical status and how long she thought he had to live and reported to me that the nurse didn't know but my husband didn't think she sounded urgent. I personally felt a sense of urgency, though. I started calling family members. I remember yelling on my mom's answering machine for her to wake up--that dad was in ICU. No one seemed to be as frantic as I was at the time. My mom said she was getting in the shower first and I was upset. "Taking a shower?" I couldn't understand why she wasn't in a panic too. I wanted my husband to come with me to the hospital, so I waited for someone to come to watch our youngest daughter. My brother told me he would come to get my daughter, so I waited outside impatiently, staring down the street. It seemed like an hour before he came, but at least he showed up. I ran into the house and got my phone and hugged my brother's girlfriend and thanked them for coming. Then, just as I stepped out the door, my mom called my cell phone, saying, "Forget going to the hospital, Julie. They just called. Your dad died."

My heart just broke into a million pieces. How could this be? In spite of trying and promising, I wasn't there to be with him, to hold his hand. I threw the phone in the air and hit the ground, screaming and crying, "No, no, no, not my dad." I was ripping the grass out of the ground while kicking and crying, asking God why he took him. Why wasn't I there with him? Why didn't I go to his side without anyone else with me? Why did I wait? Why? Why?

Now, all of us then ran off to the hospital to be with Dad and to demand some answers. When we arrived, we asked to speak to his doctor and we were told someone would call us. None of us could understand how we could have him picked up for treatment, put in a hospital under court-mandated treatment, and now he was dead. What had happened to the treatment? We had done it to save our dad's life, and now he was dead. We were all wondering what the hell was going on. I couldn't help thinking that the hospital didn't take care of him properly and they just put him in some room to let him die alone. I remember asking the nurse if anyone was there—a chaplain perhaps--to pray for him, and she said no. I was able to let that go, since I know I prayed for him that night. My uncle called me, asking what had happened to dad and none of us knew. I was just crying uncontrollably, trying to understand what had happened too. My uncle was alone in a hotel room in Illinois, waiting for our dad to arrive, and now all the news was is that he had passed away. We were all in disbelief with our hearts broken. We went to see our dad one last time in his hospital bed. As he was lying there in the bed, I'll never forget how he looked so peaceful and even several years younger. His serene appearance was unbelievable and hard to comprehend. There was our dad -a man who went through so much in his life and in an instant he left this world behind. No real good-byes or farewell, just gone. I soon called the hospital chaplain to the room for a final prayer. The family gathered around his bed and we bowed our heads and prayed. I know this would have made our dad proud--to see all of his kids there with him, loving him and praying for him and us. Later we would learn that he died due to an upper gastrointestinal bleed and his esophagus ruptured. Another contributor listed was chronic ethanolism. It wasn't supposed to end this way, but if he hadn't died here near us then, he would have died while traveling to be with his brother. That missed flight was a good thing in only that way.

After we left the hospital, I drove to my mom's and we went through his briefcase where he placed all of his important documents and laid across the very bottom was the note that I left him in his motel door, just days before. It was comforting to know that he saw and kept the letter, as it told him how much I loved him. As I opened his wallet, the "Sinners Prayer" was there. At the top of it, I had written, "Please read it as often as you can." At the bottom, I had written that he was never alone. Although my dad was in the hospital without us when he died, I know that he knew he wasn't alone. The Lord and his angels were there and took him home, taking all of his pain and suffering away.

As a small last tribute to my dad, a card arrived from the bank where he had recently opened an account. It was a personal note from one of the Bankers, saying what a pleasure it was to meet him and that she had really enjoyed his sense of humor and that it was nice to have customers who made her smile. It made me smile to read the note. Even in such an everyday transaction, dad left his impression on people.

We held a small but pleasant funeral service in Florida for our dad, followed by burial in Wisconsin with his family and friends. Dad did get his royal flush as he and my husband planned. My brother delivered a beautiful eulogy about our dad's life and even shared a story about dad's selfless acts of helping others. He told a story about a time when our dad was stranded somewhere out west and how he met a woman with her children who too were stranded and destitute at a gas station. Her car was broke down. Dad won some money on a slot machine with his last spare change. This enabled dad to stay there caring and looking out for the family until her help arrived. Dad was in luck shortly after her departure as he hitched a ride with a trucker headed to Wisconsin, which was where he wanted to go. This must have been a God thing.

My brother said our dad was a person who would give his shirt off his back if someone needed it. He talked about what a great friend our dad was to others and what a great father he was to his kids.

On our way to Wisconsin, we picked up our uncle who was just days before, waiting for our dad to arrive. I gave him some of our dad's ashes for him to send down the Wolf River, as he and my dad always promised each other they would do. He kept his promise and fulfilled his wishes.

Chapter Six: Aftermath

Our dad was buried in the same cemetery as his mom-my grandma and several other family members. I couldn't believe my worst fear had come true: the man I loved so much was now gone. No one loves me the way he loved me. I wished to have another chance to let him know how much I loved him. I remembered dad asking me one day if I would be okay after he left. I really didn't want to think about it at that time. If I could go back, I would tell him that I wouldn't be okay without him, but he would continue to live through me in my heart, and I would see him again in the end and we would be together in heaven. There's not a day that goes by that I don't think of my dad wishing he was here with his family. Often, I wonder if I made a mistake for trying to help him with the things that I done to stop him from drinking. I feel lost at times with many regrets to ponder for the rest of my own life.

Losing dad caused the world to stop turning for me. I was in a dreamlike confusion, questioning how other people were still going about their lives normally. I wonder now if it is a little like a veteran returning from Vietnam. People say that soldiers dream of nothing else but going home, but when they get home things aren't as great as they thought they would be. Things don't always taste as good as they remembered, and sometimes even the love isn't enough to take away the burning and searing memories of war.

That was how I felt. We had just lost my dad for goodness sake! It was the end of my world. When you grieve for someone that much, it is hard to take pleasure in life again for a while. It is hard to see people doing normal, everyday things and feel they are the same as you, after what you have been through. He was a remarkable person, who is greatly missed by everyone who knew him.

After returning home from burying dad, still searching for answers, I went to the doctor's office—the doctor I spoke to the night before he died--and asked why she hadn't called me back as she had promised. Why didn't she tell me my dad had taken a serious turn for the worse? I wasn't given an opportunity to be with him when he died. He deserved more than this! I told the doctor that I loved my dad and we were just trying to help him and now he was gone. She really had nothing more to say to me. No apologies or any explanation. I also went to the hospital seeking answers and wanted to know why there was no doctor to talk to our family after our dad passed away. Was there no doctor on duty at the time of his death? I never received any real answers from any of the hospital staff. I called dad's personal doctor because he was never called when my dad was hospitalized. Even his personal doctor was upset and frustrated over the situation. Evidently, he'd had a bad experience with this hospital before? According to dads medical records I discovered that he refused most of the treatment offered. The treatment offered could have possibly temporarily sustained his life. Was he really ready to go? Would he of accepted the medical treatment if I was there with him? Regretfully, I'll never know those answers.

I went to the annex to make sure no one there hurt my dad. I was assured nothing happened to him there. I was told that he didn't belong in there, and that he belonged in the hospital due to being so sick. I found out later that he was hemorrhaging at their facility within the matter of a few hours. Damn, I really hate that he was so sick and that he faced death alone. I should have been by his side to comfort him!!!!

I returned to counseling for several months as I struggled with regrets and depression over his death. I remember telling my therapist that I felt as if I had just experienced the saddest story ever told in losing my dad. I considered dying myself and even contemplated suicide many times. I could not tolerate the constant pain. I felt hopeless and living a life without him anymore seemed impossible. How can I grow old without my dad? Is he waiting for me in heaven? Why did he have to die? Is he disappointed in me? The grief was so apparent that I almost lost my job. I would have moments of sadness and start crying uncontrollably. My boss at the time actually told me to straighten up or disciplinary action would be taken.

Clearly, my boss never endured a loss like mine!

I had a dream after dad passed, where I was at the hospital flipping through a book trying to find my dad's room. I was crying out to him and telling dad that I was going to find him. When I awoke, I was devastated that his death was real. It was like hearing the news all over again. I lay in bed crying out for him for some time. I just couldn't believe he was gone.

I guess I'm still hanging on to all my memories with dad, still searching for closure. Unable to let go, I still keep his packed suitcase stored away, his chair, table, other personal items and the last set of bloodstained clothes he wore. It took me over five years to throw away two frozen steaks that he gave my husband the week of his death. Maybe there is no time that will completely heal me? I even saved dad's last voice mail messages on a recorder which I thought were important to share but they are still so painful for me to read or hear:

Monday 4:03 p.m. - "Hi, Julie it's just dad."

Just dad!

"I didn't mean to hang up on you. This phone will only stay on hold for a while then shut itself off. So I know you're busy right now but when you get a chance, just call me back. Okay?"

He was concerned that I would think he hung up on me! I had told him that when I was at work, he could call me any time and I would leave work if he needed me to.

Thursday 9:17 a.m. - "Hi, honey, it's Dad. When you get a chance, Julie, will you give me a call? You don't have to be in a hurry or anything."

I was at work when he left this message. His voice was shaky, as if he had been upset, maybe even crying?

The next call reflects dad under the influence of alcohol. It shows his guilt (which I'm told by Alcoholics Anonymous is one of the strongest, and most deeply buried, emotions alcoholics feel). It also shows that, even when he was almost incapacitated with alcohol, he thought about others and also about family.

Thursday 12:51 p.m. - "It's your asshole dad. Give me a call when you get this." (Coughing noise in the background. Someone was telling dad his taxi was there. My guess it was a bartender. My dad never hung up on this call, so I captured his time in the bar as he left in a taxi. He was intoxicated at this point.)

Dad yelled to ask everyone if they were okay and said, "All right, then, I gotta go. Oh, hey, yeah, thanks, thank you, thank you. Come give me a hug, 'cause I gotta go. I'll see you guys." In the background I heard a lady say, "Be careful," to which my dad replied, "Oh, I'm fine. I'm fine."

As he got in the taxi he spoke to the driver and said, "Hey, little lady. Do you have any kids"? She replied "Yep. Do you have any kids?" Dad said yes and that she had five of them, good, oh good. She asked him where he was going and he said, "I don't know yet." She said, "You don't know yet!" Then he struggled to tell her where to go. He told her it was a place down over the bridge, where his daughter lived (it was my home). Then the call ended. He dialed back then.

Thursday 12:54 p.m - "Julie, this is your dad. I can't think of that name of that little place up there around the corner from where you live. So you have to call me right back, because I have the poor girl captive in a taxi cab. Okay?

Call me right back!"

Thursday 12:57 p.m. - "Hey, Julie, when you get a second, call Daddy. I kidnapped, I kidnapped, I kidnapped this girl that was driving a cab. She's married and has kids, so I can't keep her long. So as soon as you get a chance, call me right back. I'll be right by your house."

Thursday 2:23 p.m.- "Julie, Julie."

(It sounded like he was looking for me.)

Thursday 2:25 p.m.- "Julie, Julie!"

(He was calling my name out loud.)

Dad's calls were becoming more frequent and urgent. My co-workers were starting to glare at me as my cell phone kept ringing. I was working in a call center and unable to answer each phone call from my dad. He seemed to want me every minute at that point. Looking back, I should of just left work to be with him. He really needed me this time!

Shortly after dad passed away, I ran into one of his old bartenders at a laundry mat

while washing some blankets, and I asked
her if she knew about my dad passing away.
She said yes, and that she had his obituary
posted on her refrigerator. She told me
that dad called her his angel. She said
that my dad was in a lot of pain and that
he seemed to be suffering. This was just a
small example of how he touched others
during his life. I hear that most drinkers
do not strike up such human relationships
with their bartenders.

I told dad shortly before he passed that
he should write a book. He appeared to
think about it, but I guess he left it for
me to do? I know dad would be pleased about
me writing this book, especially, if
sharing his life can help others. I've had
several dreams with him since he passed
away and in one of them he told me that he

was proud of me and I was headed in the right direction. This was when I first requested his military records to start my research. This dream inspired me to really move forward with this book.

Still looking for more answers, I decided to call the Veterans Administration to question some of the findings in dad's medical records dated 1988. I called to tell them they made a misdiagnosis of him having a personality disorder NOS, which I found was a common error. I told the VA Rep that I conducted a lot of research and I know he was suffering from Post-Traumatic Stress Disorder. I asked the Rep, "How did you all miss this?" "How did we miss this?" I told him that I was writing a book about my dad's life and PTSD was clearly what my dad suffered from and he sought help for it over 16 years ago, but he was misdiagnosed. Before we ended the phone call the caring Rep asked for dad's service number so he could review more information and maybe he could tell me something that I didn't already know. I was wondering what else could he inform me? I already obtained his military records and medical records. He then said that my dad had another record on file. I couldn't believe what I just heard. Unbelievable….He told me that dad submitted a claim for PTSD which, was DENIED! Oh my God!!! I responded in disbelief "Wait! He filed a claim"? I asked when it was denied. He did not have the information available but, would request a copy for me since, the file was never destroyed. There is a Freedom Act in place to protect the files. He told me that all records after the late

1990's were entered electronically. I
started to cry at this point. I couldn't
believe that my dad was aware of PTSD.

Something that none of his children knew!
I kept saying," I can't believe it" I can't
believe it" at least a hundred times. I
felt confused emotionally. I sort of felt
comfort in knowing that he was aware of
what he was suffering from but, felt anger
that he was denied the compensation and
failed treatment which led him to continue
to medicate himself with alcohol. PTSD was
his secret and the government did not
recognize his trauma. He kept the claim to
himself. The government gave up on him, so
he gave up too. Shame-Shame-Shame. No
veteran should have to fight to receive
benefits. I requested a copy of his claim
so I could seek more answers. My dad was

truly suffering from the effects of war and this was his thanks-NOTHING. The Veterans hospital releases my father back in 1988 with a wrong diagnosis, personality disorder NOS instead of the truth. After 10 days, he exceeded his stay and is sent to seek help in his local community. Was this a mistake? Did he just accidentally get overlooked? Was this to prevent him from receiving a service-connected disability or an attempt to save money? Nothing else makes sense.

I received dads denied claim and uncovered that he admitted himself again, 10 years later for treatment. It was now March 10, 1998 and he sought help for his alcohol addiction which he said was getting out of hand. My older brother convinced him that he ought to do something about it now.

He admitted to being a binge drinker for 28 years, following his Vietnam war experience. He told them that he had trouble with personal relationships, anxiety -especially in crowds of people, and usually drinks when he anticipates social settings, sleep disturbances, socially isolated, anger control problems, "thoughts of Vietnam", avoids anything about Vietnam, otherwise has problems sleeping. He said he was with the 557th Engineers in Vang Tau and Ta Nein Vietnam and experienced rocket mortars. He stated he went all over the northern area of Vietnam and was in multiple defoliated areas. He did not spray any chemicals himself or do any spraying. He was a heavy equipment operator and moved multiple defoliated underbrush jungle trees and what not. He told them about the mine explosion and it damaged his hearing. He was not severely hurt in the mine explosion which, blew up his tractor that he was driving. He said that he had a dermal rash afterwards, and after Nam he had an occasional flare up of lesions, but no further issues.

He stated that he awakes several times during the night. Sometimes awakes to night sweats and a pounding pulse. Dad says he was in the bush over in Vietnam and he lost friends. He has some dreams and invasive thoughts. He stays away from combat movies. He sometimes dreams of the Vietnam experience. He likes to position himself where he can see the door. In the early years he complained about the blowing of the fire whistle in Wabeno, Wisconsin where he lived as it created an extreme startling response. He said shortly after leaving the military service he had been active and engaging in frequent fighting. He experienced trouble controlling violent behavior in his life shortly after military service. His medical record was stated that he was being referred to PTSD treatment. He was referred to group therapy sessions with four other Vietnam veterans having difficulty staying sober ever since their in country experiences. One man in particular discussed his first fire fight, and his fear carrying a wounded soldier to safety amid blood curdling cries of pain. Another member shared how he read everything he could find about Vietnam, particularly books which related closely to what he did there. Another member questioned what good was telling of stories because, "what could anyone do about it anyway", especially about the persons killed in combat. (In my opinion, that was my dad's response.) A fourth member was tearful and described tears being to "fear" but could not identify further any specifics he was willing to share.

Following the group session dad spoke with the therapist privately and said he wanted to leave early. He didn't understand what good it would do to share combat experiences. He stated his experiences were unlike the experiences shared in group. He felt like an outsider looking in. He then shared some of the experiences. The therapist noted that he was not alone in with dealing with this burden and other vets experienced similar circumstances and that if he shared he would come to realize that he was not alone. The therapist did not document the specific burden on his medical records, which makes me wonder what dad told her?

When dad returned to the group session, he basically ended up telling the group that he was not ready to talk about his war experiences. He was not comfortable talking about his trauma and even broke out into hives due to the overwhelming stress.

After several weeks, he did complete the treatment program successfully and was encouraged to attend Alcohol Anonymous meetings and obtain a sponsor to assist with the recovery process. He was informed that Cognitive Processing Therapy (CPT) counseling was available to him afterwards. This type of therapy is designed to help Veterans understand how to change how they think about their trauma and its aftermath, as well as recognizing what thoughts cause stress and make symptoms worse. Veterans learn ways to cope with feelings such as anger, guilt and fear. I do not believe that my dad attended anymore counseling sessions, but I do know that he stopped drinking for a while around that time. Unfortunately, he would start drinking again soon, which I believe was after he received his denial letter from the Department of Veterans Affairs. They sent him a denial letter for having PTSD in November 1998. The letter stated that they did not find the following condition to be service connected. They wanted more evidence regarding his claim. I believe that with all of the documentation they received, his claim could not get any clearer. They stated that there was no evidence to show that he engaged in combat with the enemy. They stated that the evidence available for review was inadequate to establish that a stressful experience occurred. Give me a break! I think that was a disgrace to make those statements. They know he was living in a combat zone facing fire every day for over 2 years and men were dying all of the time. Just look at the photographs and review the statistics! Visit the Vietnam Veterans Memorial wall for a list of casualties. Did dad participate in several weeks of PTSD treatment for nothing? Why would he be referred to PTSD treatment if he did not have PTSD?

Being concerned, I took all of dad's records, documents and photographs to a local VA Rep and I told them that I wanted to resubmit his denied claim. I was given the paperwork to fill out, to submit on my own. The VA Rep stated that my dad had the responsibility to follow up on his claim and continue treatment. If you ask me the treatment route failed for him and I think he should have been compensated without having to fight and keep reliving his experience in therapy sessions. Did they really not trust he was suffering from PTSD? I sure believe there's a personal responsibility for our Government to take care of our men and women when they are traumatized for the rest of their lives after serving our great country. What happens when there is NO effective treatment plan that works for our veterans?

Maybe too many years passed by without receiving the treatment that my dad needed?

Perhaps he was too far gone when he came for help again 10 years later?

I must say that I do really appreciate that the VA healthcare system was available for my dad to receive medical care throughout his life, but I'm very disappointed that he was denied any compensation. I know he worked very hard all of his life and he would NEVER apply for something that he didn't think he was worthy to receive. No way!

Feeling uneasy and wanting another opinion, I went to the local Department of Veterans Affairs to request my dad's claim be reopened. This time I was more prepared and I included a timeline of events related to my dad's illnesses and Vietnam experience. I provided a lot of documentation and research which included several obituaries from other Vietnam Veterans who have died an early death post-Vietnam. Surprisingly, when I received dad's service records the VA mistakenly mailed me a list of other Veteran names with their social security numbers. I was able to research the names easily online and find obituaries that show several 50 to 60 year old men who died of natural cause's post-Vietnam. Really makes me wonder if they died trying to get help too? I provided names of men who lost their lives during the Vietnam War conflict that were associated with dads unit as proof that he experienced stressors. I didn't know what else to do at this point. Shortly, after the visit I received a letter that basically stated my dad would have had to of died from certain Agent Orange diseases and illnesses, like cancer, diabetes, lung, heart and other issues, not because of a veterans misconduct as a result of abusing alcohol and drugs. In order, to obtain a VA rating of service-connection for death it will be necessary to obtain more medical documentation to prove another illness and then obtain an amended death certificate. I believe this VA Rep did all that he could do personally to assist me. I easily connected with this Rep, because he too served in Vietnam. I left there thinking that he would have helped me further if it was in his power.

Unfortunately, I am required to provide additional medical evidence. I guess a mental illness-PTSD is not recognized as a valid contributor to a cause of death. I believe that dad having PTSD was certainly the number one reason for his death. This is an illness created by trauma and it's REAL! I cannot give up on this issue and I will continue to research this matter and pursue reopening his claim at a later time. I'm still alive!!!! Where do I go now with this? Who can help me?

I will not give up on my dad!

Chapter Seven: Never Forgotten

My dad's last birthday wish was for his family to find happiness in this life. I must say that dad may have left this world early, but he did live his life his way and the best that he could. I think my dad drank for comfort and he lived his life as abundantly as he could while battling PTSD and alcoholism. Through this tragedy, he has certainly inspired me to help others more and more. I want all Vietnam Veterans to know that they are not forgotten. If any veteran of any war is struggling with stress or addictions, do seek professional help somewhere. A lot of communities have local veteran associations or organizations to provide direct support or services. The Veterans Administration has more available resources than I've ever seen before. Alcoholic Anonymous is a great resource. There is helpful online support too. Just do something!! Don't give up on seeking help!

Personally, I have met many great people through different Veterans organizations. In some way they have helped me get through my own difficult times dealing with the loss of my dad. I remember meeting another Vietnam Veteran at an event one day and I spoke about dads passing and shared that he had PTSD. Our conversation was really brief and I soon walked away. Before I left the event, he came up to me again and asked for a hug. Of course, I said, "yes", and he hugged me and said with a trembling voice, "that was for your dad". I was speechless as I walked away and soon broke down myself. What a caring, loving person he was to do that for my dad! A healing experience for me!

Other Vietnam Veterans tell me to be proud of my dad no matter what and I agree 100% with them. I will always defend those who serve our country and I am extremely proud to be a daughter of a Vietnam Veteran.

Some facts about alcoholism and Post-Traumatic Stress Disorder from the U.S. Department of Veteran Affairs:

http://ncptsd.va.gov/ncmain/ncdocs/fact_shts/fs
alcohol.html

The majority of Vietnam Veterans who seek
treatment for Post-Traumatic Stress
Disorders have serious problems with
alcohol. Older veterans are at increased
risk for suicide if they are alcoholics as
well as suffering from PTSD. War veterans
tend to be binge drinkers. A binge may be
triggered by memories of traumatic events
brought on more vividly by current life
events that remind the veteran of thoughts,
sights, sounds, smells or feelings
experienced during combat.

Alcohol provides momentary relief from
stress. However, it works against the
veteran in a number of ways. It hampers
natural enjoyment of life, which is healing
to the traumatized veteran. It may

interfere with employment, adding financial stress to the veteran's life. It also plays havoc with personal relationships, which are a strong source of satisfaction and happiness in life.

Veterans often shut off their emotions so as not to feel the pain they experience so intensely. Alcohol adds to this numbing effect. It can also add to anger, loneliness, depression and hyper-vigilance— a feeling of always needing to be on one's guard. In all these ways, including and especially the last—hyper-vigilance, or not feeling safe—the veteran continues to re-traumatize him- or herself.

PTSD is often characterized by nightmares about being back in the combat experience. The use of alcohol seems to decrease the severity and number of nightmares. However, it adds to sleeplessness and, if the person gives up alcohol, the nightmares come right back.

In short, alcoholism masks trauma and postpones getting over it. It offers, however, short, temporary respite from the emotional and mental pain of the severe trauma of being in a war.

The National Archives report that the U.S. Military suffered 58,220 casualties with eight of the casualties being women.

The highest casualties occurred between the years of 1967-1969.

According to a study I found on www.history.com it reveals that 91% of Vietnam Veterans say that they are glad they served and 74% said they would serve again even knowing the outcome. The study also states that 85% of Vietnam Veterans made a successful transition to civilian life. I know without a doubt that my dad was proud to have served our country and he would do it all over again without hesitation.

"Thank you to all who serve or who have served our great country."

God Bless

Vietnam Photos 1968-1970

Another 357th Engineer

NEVER FORGOTTEN

In memory of my Hero- my Dad,

Julius "Jerry" Duane Weber

Day is done, gone the sun,

from the lakes

from the hills

from the sky.

All is well,

safely rest,

God is nigh

"Taps"

ABOUT THE AUTHOR

Following the loss of my father on October 8, 2005, I was inspired to research my dad's Vietnam experience to create understanding about his life and struggles with Post-Traumatic Stress Disorder.

A Daughter's Hero was written to raise awareness about the long lasting effects of war and shares the unconditional love and compassion between a daughter and father.

Cover art and design by; Samantha K. Weber, Granddaughter of Julius "Jerry" Weber

Special thanks to my family and friends. I appreciate your support and encouragement.

Contact Author:

Email: adaughtershero@yahoo.com

Website: www.adaughtershero.com

34146676R00142

Made in the USA
Charleston, SC
02 October 2014